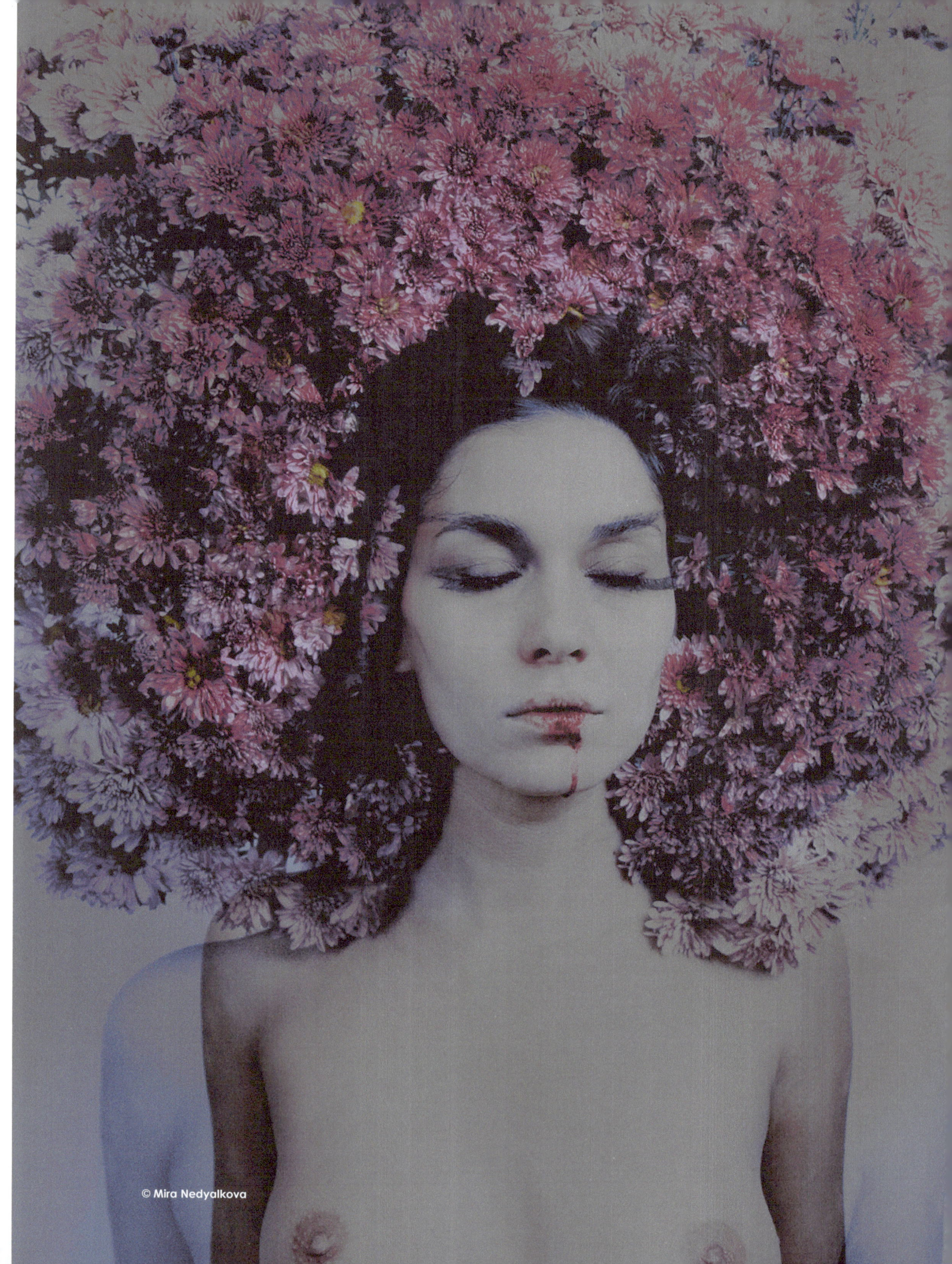

Letter from the Publisher

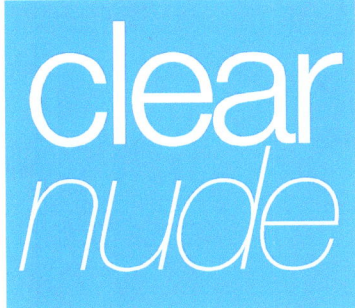

the lens + the nude

Allicette Torres
**Publisher &
Creative Director**

Karen Rayne
Associate Editor

Contributors
Alessandro Saponi
Anoush Anou
ASP
Brian Lynch
Brwax
Carmin Conner
David Bainbridge
Eli Dijkers
Feliz Paloma Gonzalez
Florent Barnades
G.W. Benard
Helene Williams
K.D. Dickson
Linda Troeller
Michael Gakuran
Mira Nedyalkova
Nicolas Gavino
Nom de Guerre
Patrick Cockpit
Pola Esther
Rober Weissner
SH Sadler
Stefan Wegmüller
T.H.Taylor
Thom Peters

Advertising
Amy Morlas
clearnude@gmail.com
646.355.8271

As we're come to the close of our final issue within our four volume series, I'm pleased to say our growing name and recognition has created a tremendous community of artists. We've been able to join together in a beautifully curated series. I'm grateful to all the artists who have shared their work and to the readers who have voiced the same excitement for this underexposed and often alienated form of art.

Moving forward, we are a bit unclear as to what the next steps are for the magazine. To speak plainly, it has been a difficult labor of love; I am at a crossroads with continuing the magazine under the current circumstances. As of now there is no assembled team. I am saddened by the state of affairs. I believe in the magazine, it's contents and what it has accomplished for the nude photography art form and it's associated community. Going forward I will need to figure out how to maintain the magazine alive in some shape way or form; whether it's publishing the magazine twice a year, having gallery exhibitions or finding some other creative way to maintain a presence.

Since its inception, Clear Nude magazine hasn't been without its share of hurdles; from general production issues, to even a select few declaring the magazine another form of pornography. Overshadowing this has been the remarkable support we've received from artists and readers alike, praising its raw beauty, honesty and unveiling of what has traditionally been perceived subversive underground art genre.

Clearly, the time had come for the unveiling of an art form that wasn't solely meant for a controversial label, but to the core is what I believe to be, the ultimate artistic expression of the human condition: tragically flawed, defiantly unique and yes, perfectly designed. Each ideal exposed, fearlessly displayed and ultimately triumphant in its surroundings.

Continuing this effort, for this issue we have a stellar roster of work by photographers such as ASP, Eli Dijkers, SH Sadler, Patrick Cockpit, Brwax, Nicolas Gavino to name a few. From a new contributing writer, Michael Gkuran, we're excited to feature the captivating history of nude Japanese pearl divers in an essay titled 'Ama's, the nude mermaids of Japan'. Another potentially provocative essay is about women, nudity and their orgasms, it's another must read.

As you explore the photographic narrative, I would like to thank you again, our readers and the hundreds of contributors for helping to make Clearnude Magazine a successful celebration of the nude photographic art form.

I can go on but I rather you explore the eclectic mix of photographers and articles in this spectacular issue.

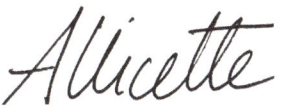

Clear Nude Magazine
Volume 1 / No. 4 Summer 2015
ISBN-13: 978-0692479384
ISBN-10: 0692479384

Published 4 times a year.

Executive, editorial and advertising
PO BOX 664,
New York, NY 10030
Phone: 646.355.8271
Email: clearnude@gmail.com
www.clearnude.com

Purchase print and digital
versions of Clear Nude
magazine via
ClearNude.com or **Amazon.com**

Printed by Amazon

the lens + the nude

Contents

ISSUE IV, SUMMER 2015

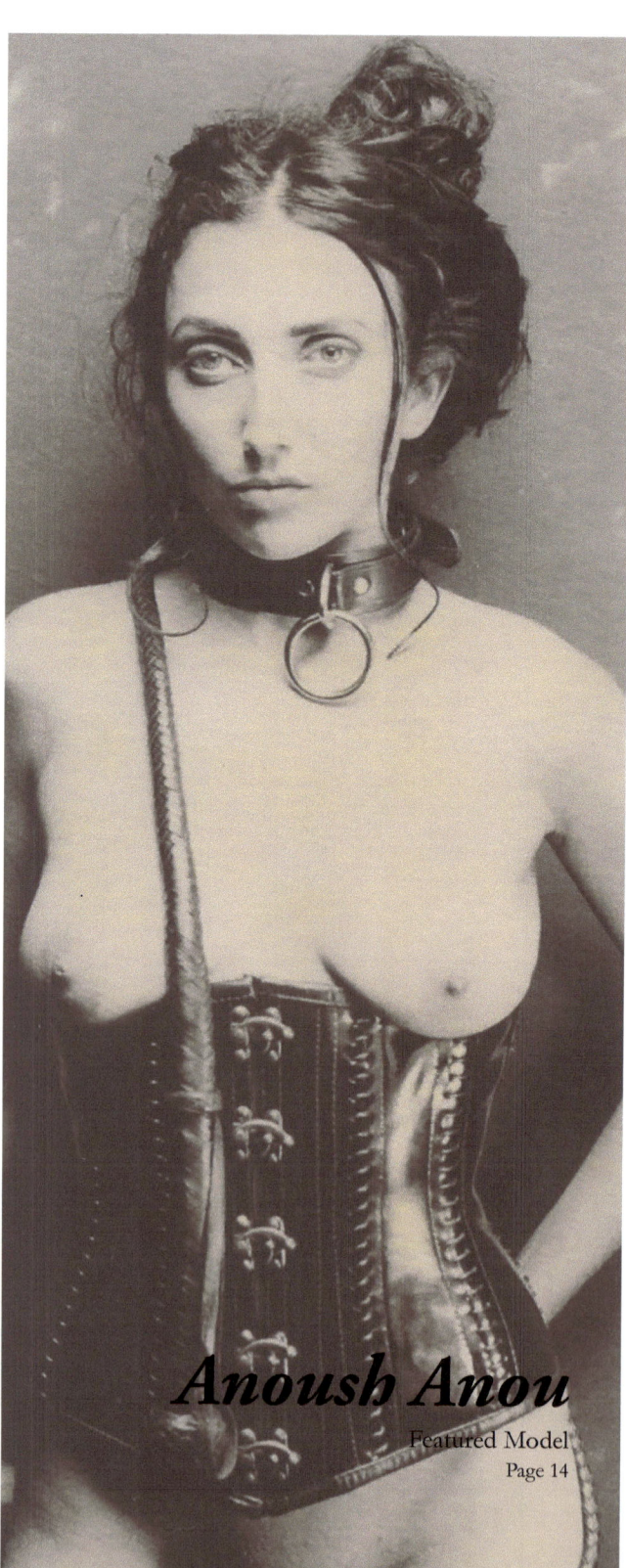

Anoush Anou

Featured Model
Page 14

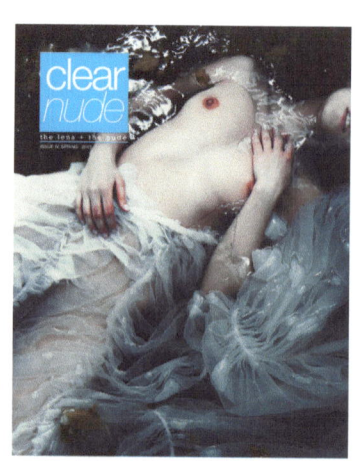

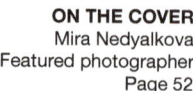

ON THE COVER
Mira Nedyalkova
Featured photographer
Page 52

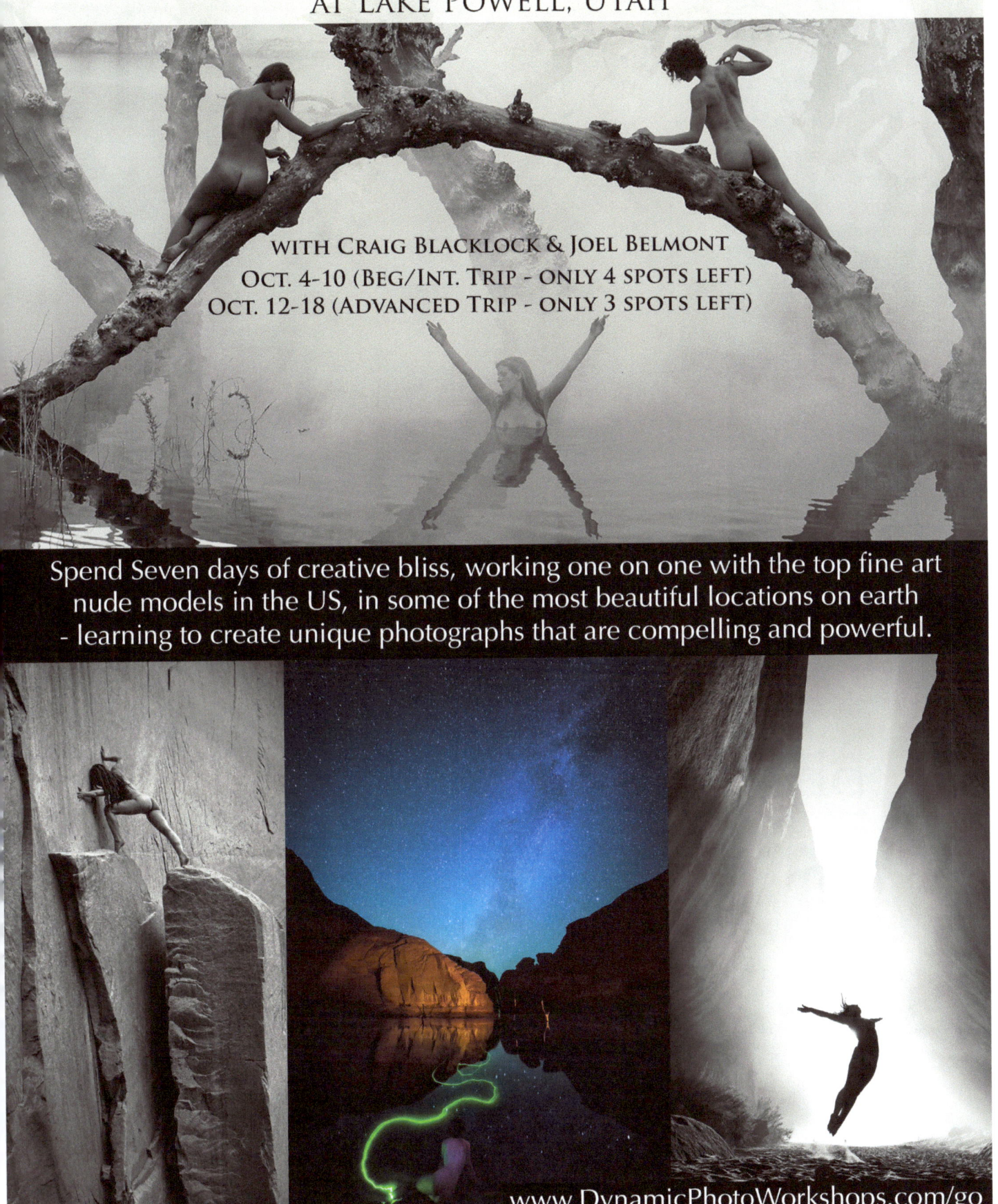

THE DYNAMIC NUDE WORKSHOP
AT LAKE POWELL, UTAH

WITH CRAIG BLACKLOCK & JOEL BELMONT
OCT. 4-10 (BEG/INT. TRIP - ONLY 4 SPOTS LEFT)
OCT. 12-18 (ADVANCED TRIP - ONLY 3 SPOTS LEFT)

Spend Seven days of creative bliss, working one on one with the top fine art nude models in the US, in some of the most beautiful locations on earth - learning to create unique photographs that are compelling and powerful.

www.DynamicPhotoWorkshops.com/go

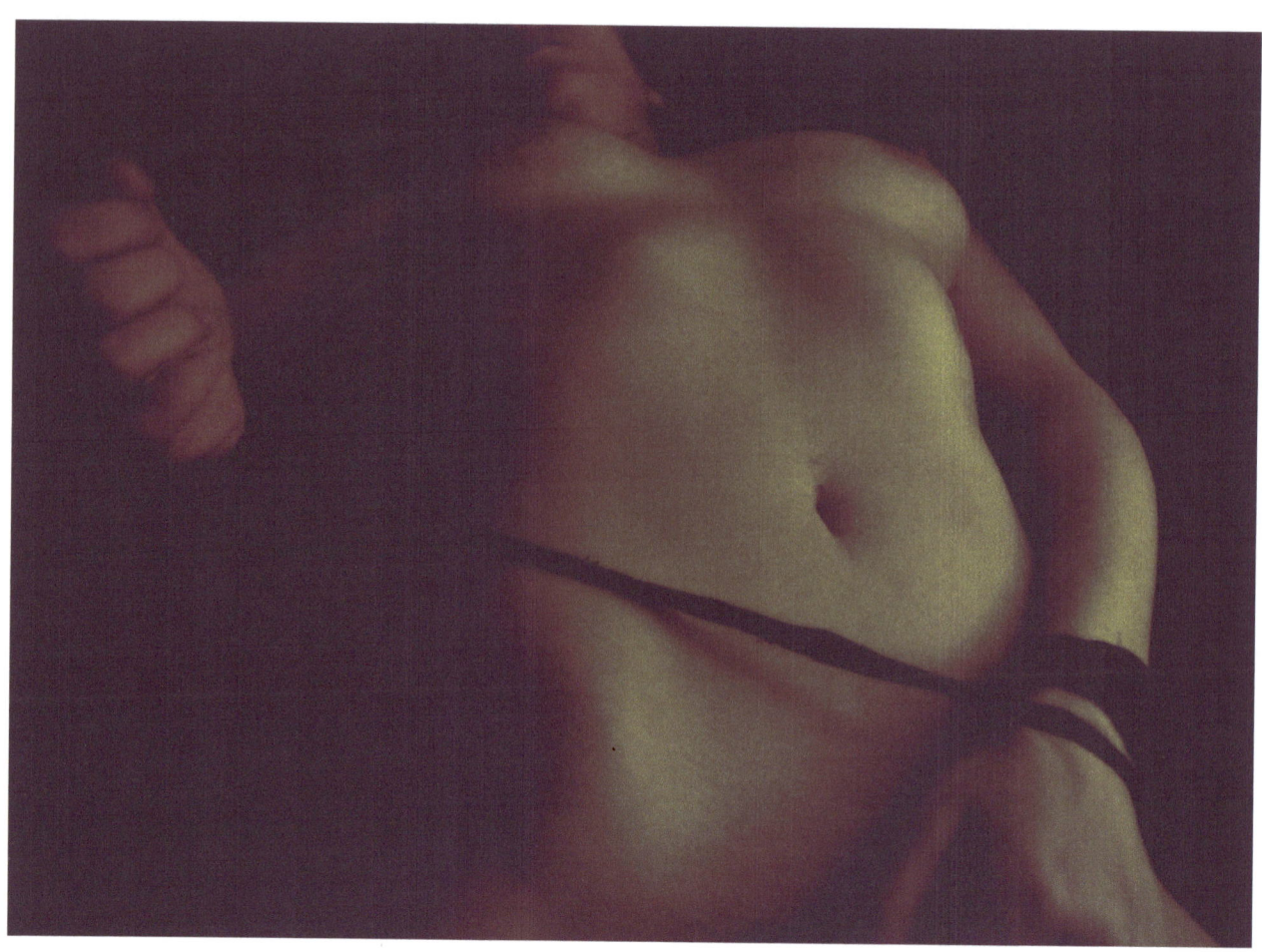

A poem &
photo story by
carmin
conner

I know that you see me,
Although you say you don't.
I write notes on the window,
In the raindrops as I float.

I know you hear my whispers,
At midnight in your bed.
I say that I still love you,
But you only turn your head.

I know you hear my footsteps,
In the hall at night I tread.
But I know that you still hear me,
Even though I am now dead. ‡

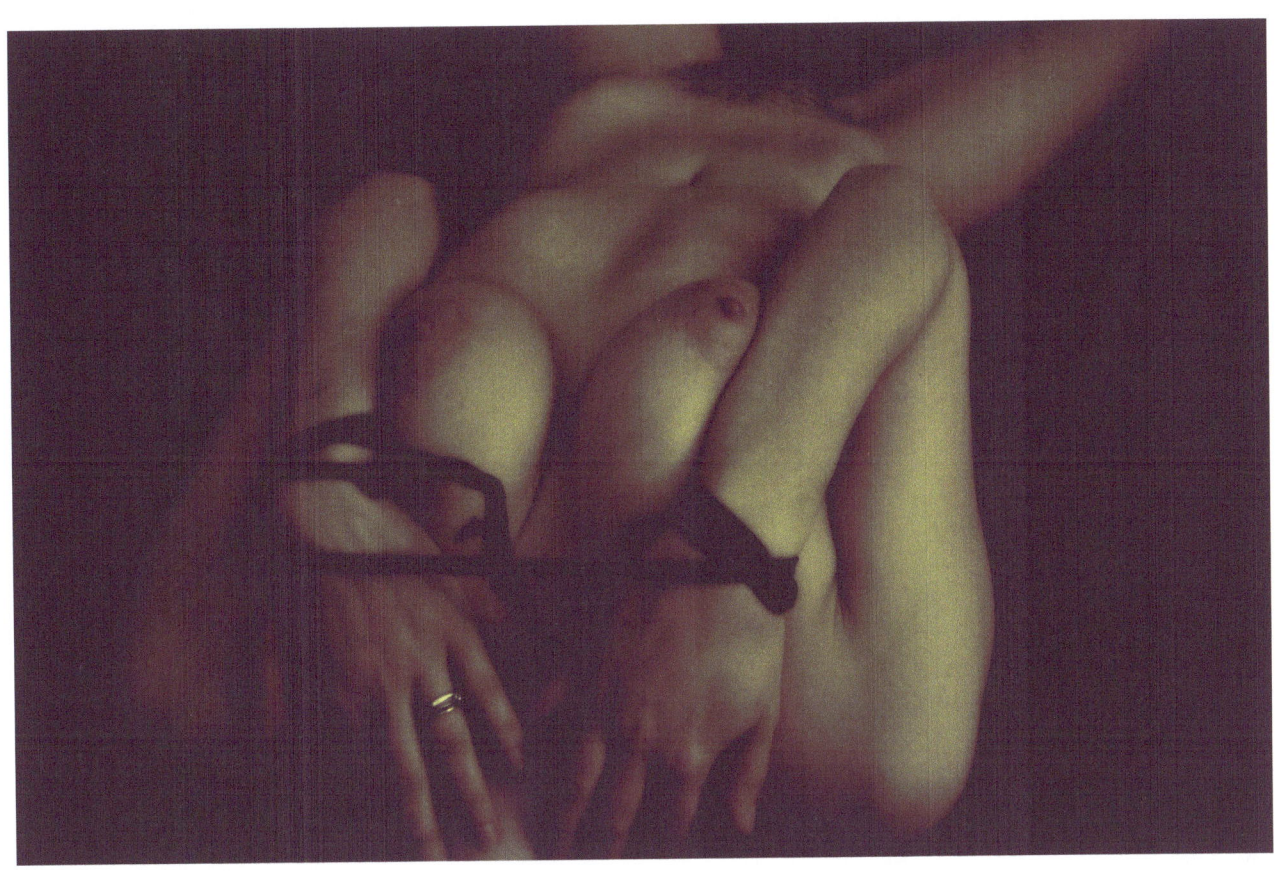

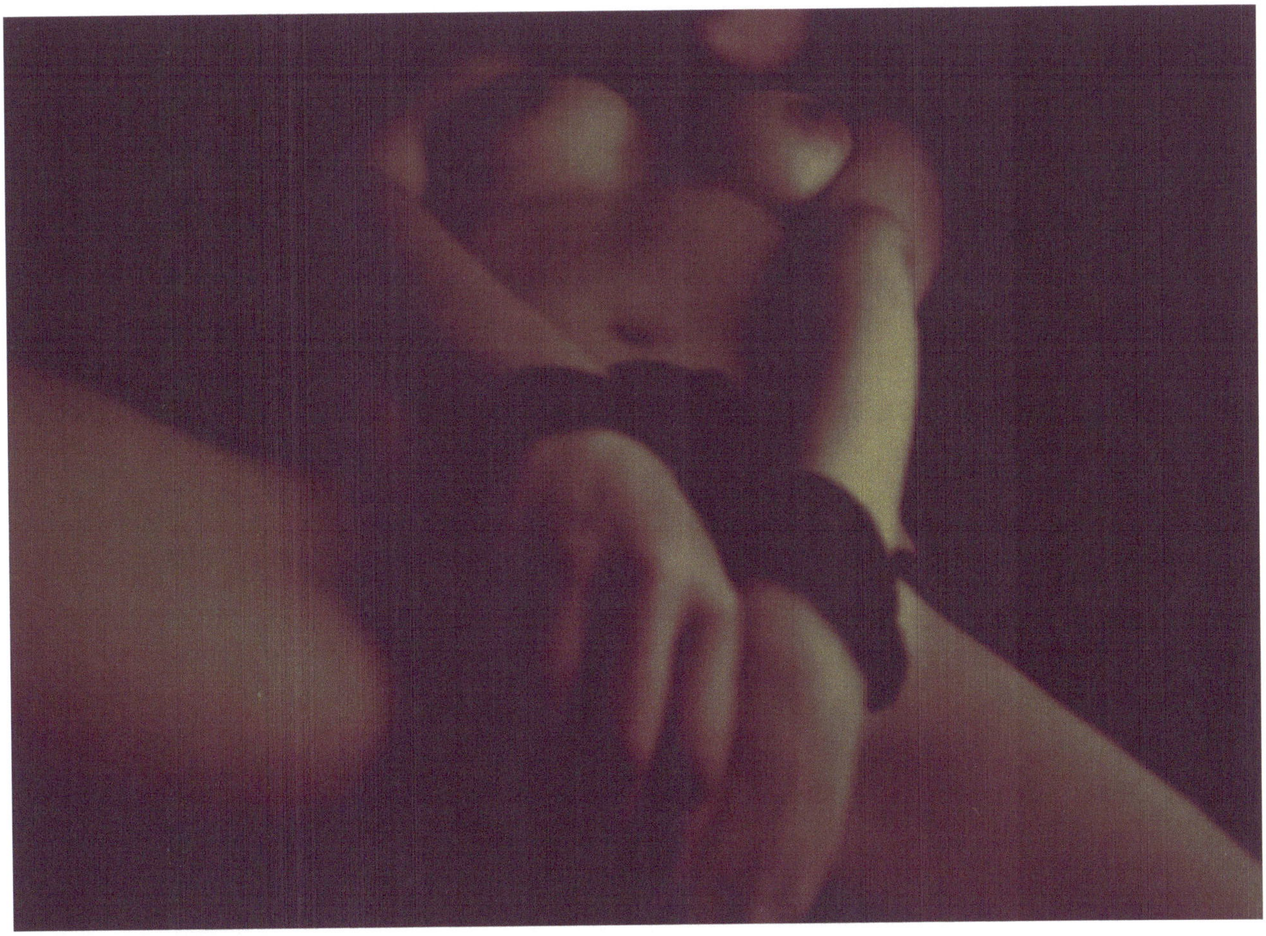

© Carmin Conner pages 6-7

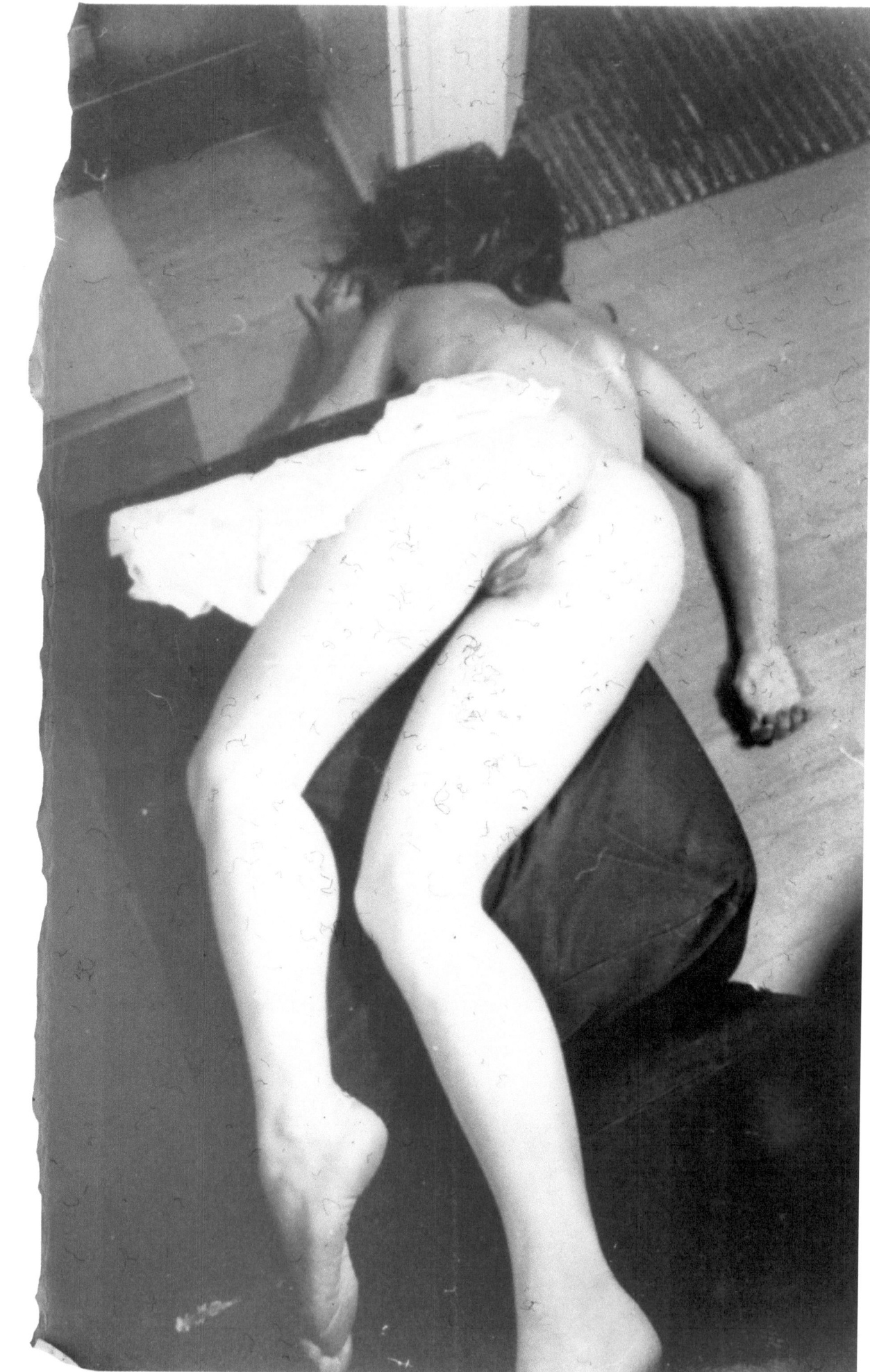

Nicolas Gavino

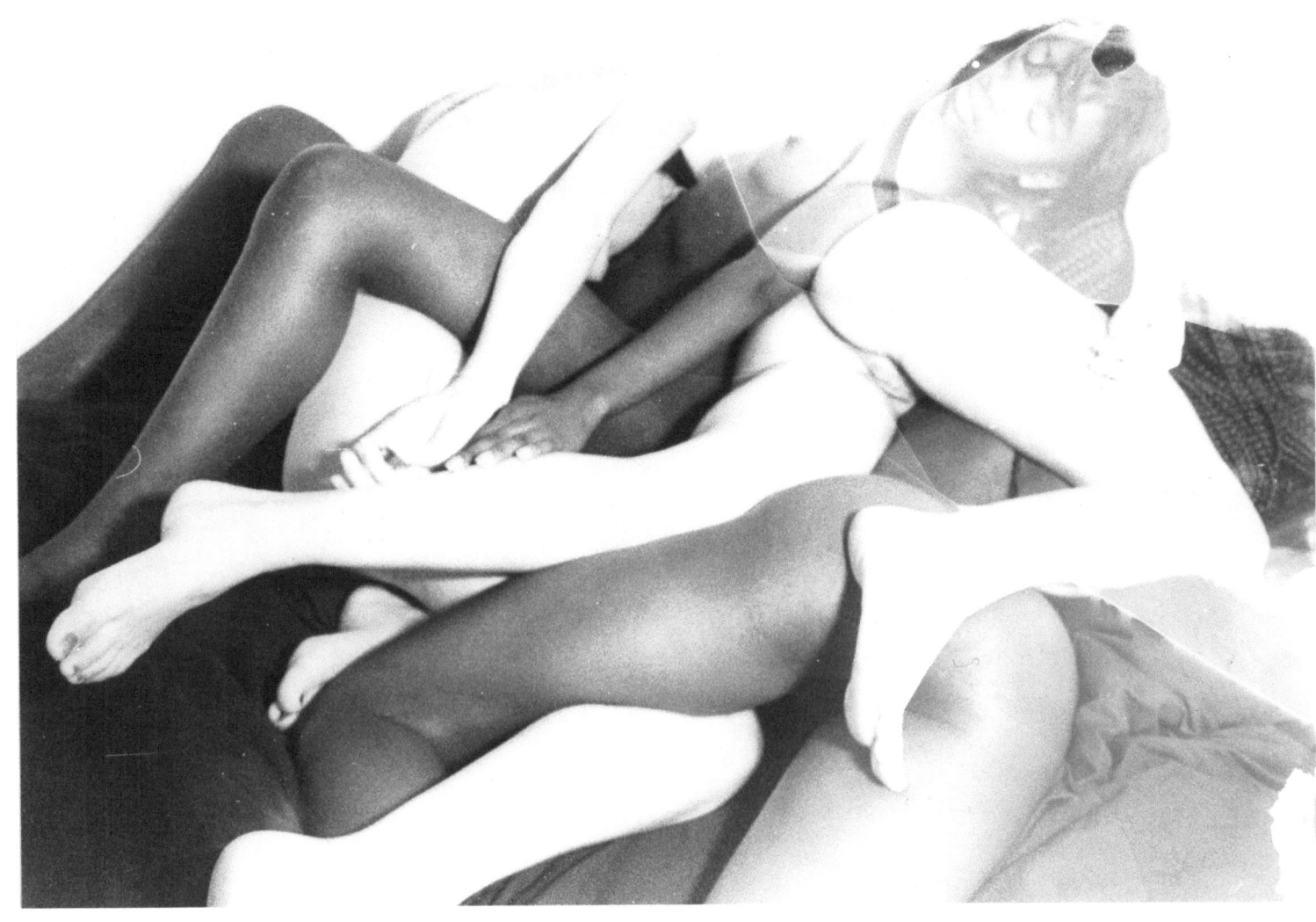

© Nicolas Gavino pages 8-10

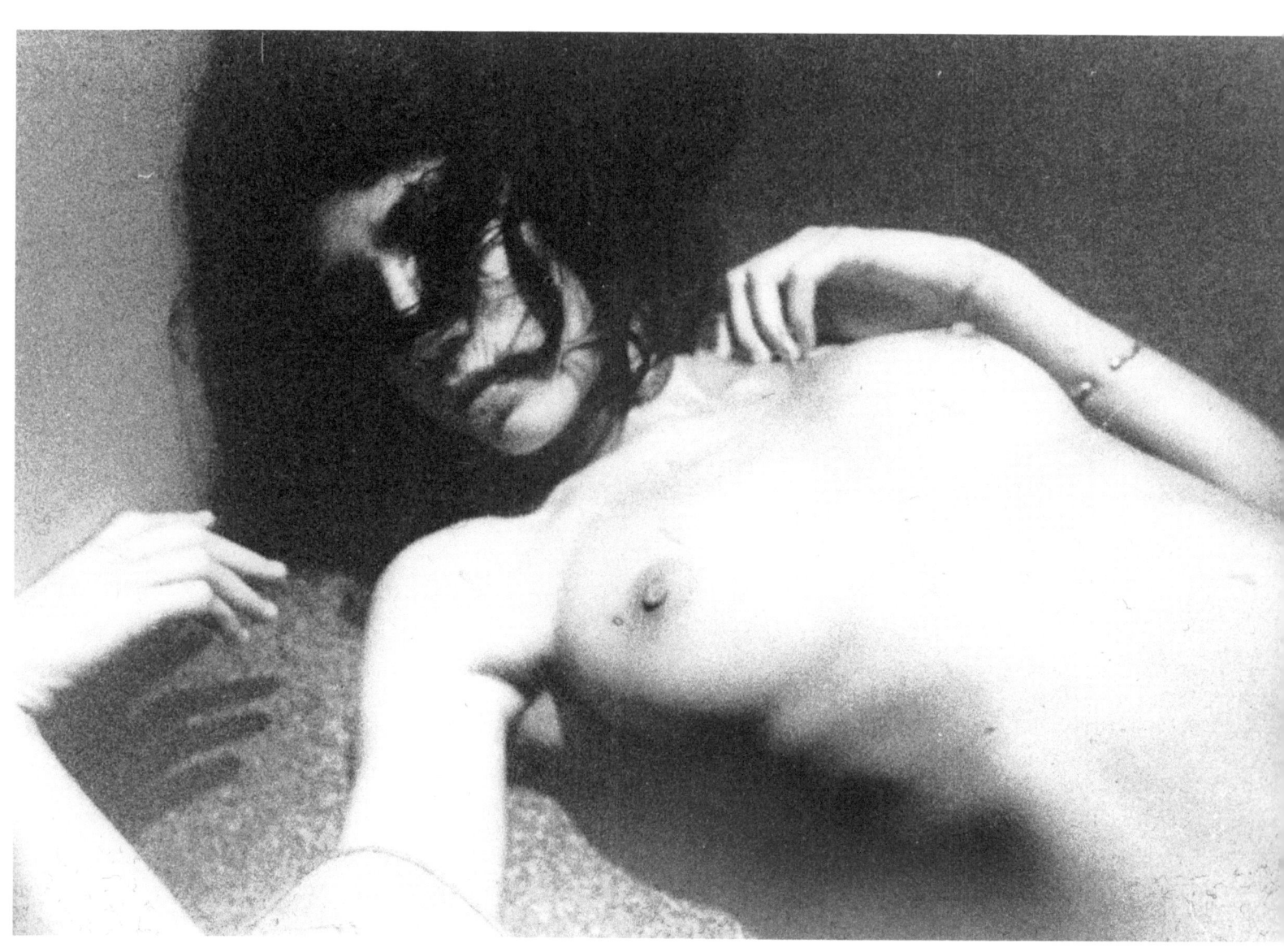

Ruminations on Nudity

by Karen Rayne

Nudity receives a response in the United States – from arousal to outrage, it is rarely left to its own quiet, independent movement through space. Even within the home, the politics of walking from the shower to the bedroom without a towel are considered with interest, or perhaps with shame if you are of a certain age, gender, or body shape. One's lack of attire in even that most intimate and private space of sleep is questioned, as if perhaps you are doing your neighbors a frightful wrong because of the slim chance that a fire will drive you into the street in a dreadfully and embarrassingly exposed state. When more than one generation is involved, the response to nudity can become shrill expressions of inherent impropriety. In shared public spaces, the sight of another human's full set of warm curves and lines can apparently cause such harm that it is legislated into small and well marked corners of space, far away from those deemed vulnerable and religious.

Regardless of their presentation as such, puritanical opinions of and restrictions to nudity are hardly universal human values. They come to us by way of our collective political ancestors, the very religious and conservative forefathers who fled persecution to find their own soil on which to follow their own beliefs and to do their own persecutions. Across many parts of Europe, Asia, Africa, and South America, the worries that emotions are tenuous, sensibilities easily offended, and identities at risk, do not overrule the possibility of the sun and air caressing our most tender of places. Other cultures do not draw hard, thick squares in art and media over women's nipples and vulvas or men's penises and color them in black, turning the entire world into their very own fear-based coloring book.

The distance that we in the United States set between ourselves and our bodies is a rejection of our deepest vulnerability and therefore our most particular beauty. There are arguments about the cognitive or emotional or psychological aspects that set humans aside from other mammals, but they all ignore the most obvious distinction: our physical bodies. It is true that we use our bodies differently than our mammalian cousins: by covering them with clothes because of our advanced (or repressed) psychological sense of shame, that we make and wield increasingly complex tools, that we have a proportionally and evolutionarily overly large brain. But why do we not acknowledge the very physical nature that affords us the ability to conceptualize and theorize about these particular differences? It is our bodies that, first and foremost, set us apart from the other animals.

We are our bodies. Rejecting or ignoring them is a foolish endeavor that only leads to the further disconnection and disintegration of our communities. Without our fleshy selves, although they offers such a bare covering for our easily injured internal organs and identities, we are merely units wandering and alone. Acknowledgements of our soft curves and lines and our needs for kind and gentle human-human touch are growing in the United States, but we are far from acceptance countrywide. One day, though, perhaps we will be whole, full, contained in our own rights rather than by layers upon layers of a false sense of control that we currently employ. And then, my friends, we will hold hands and run through the bluebonnets together. And we can approach a way of being that is right and whole. ‡

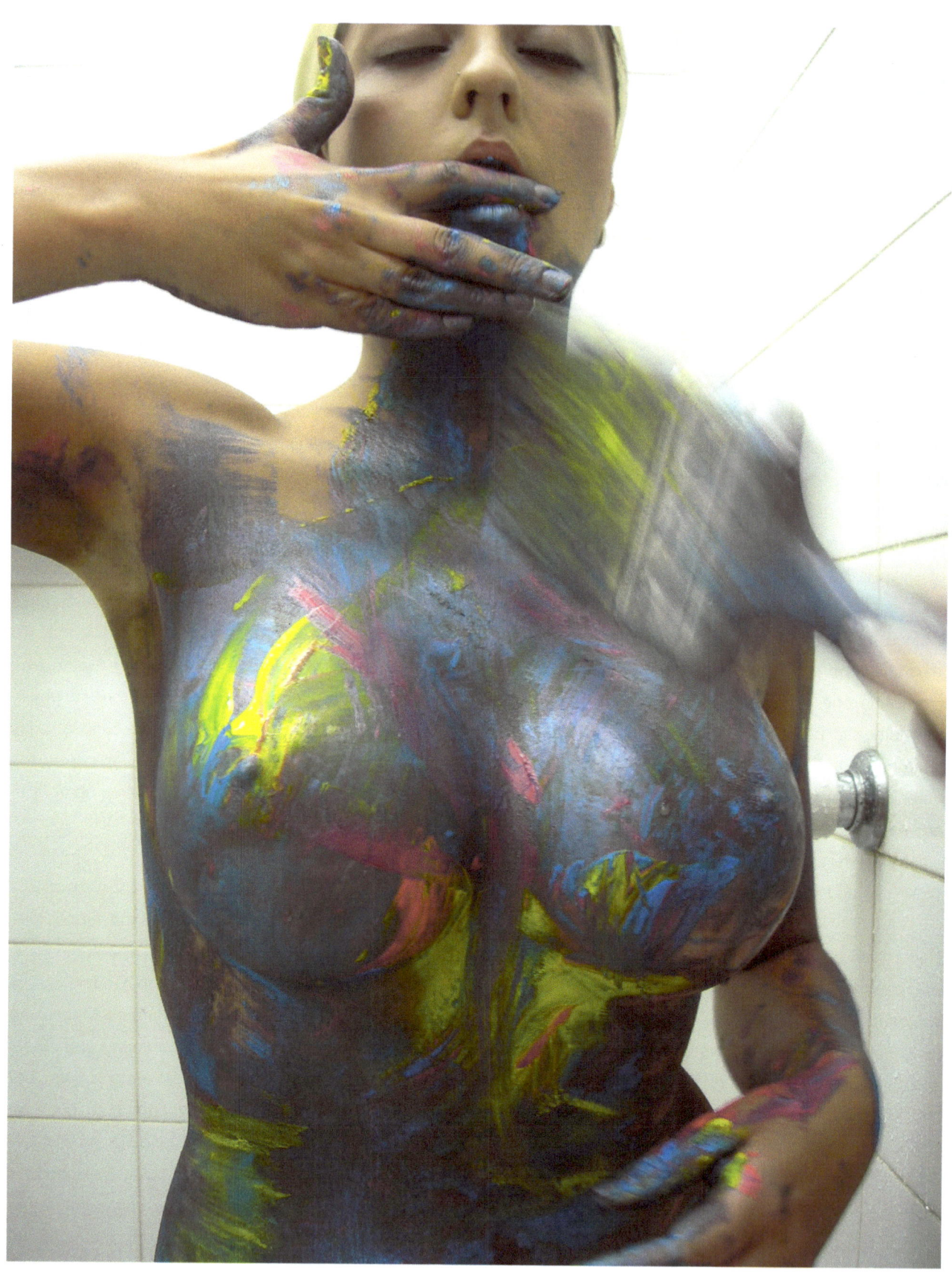

Maria, Colombia BY LINDA TROELLER from book Orgasm Photographs and Interviews, Daylight, 2014

ORGASM PHOTOGRAPHS AND INTERVIEWS

by Helene Williams
& Allicette Torres

Masturbation as an erotic subject had been a magnet for interest and fascination for centuries. The photographer Linda Troeller has tackled the subject visually in her book, "Orgasm Photographs and Interviews." In her project she interviewed women of different ages, nationalities, cultures, and sexualities from straight, bi- to lesbians and pan-sexuals, as well as sex workers; their ages ranging from 18 to 88. She created a visual dialogue about this maligned subject.

Exploring Linda's work, art psychotherapist Helene Williams, discusses below the project further by selecting a specific image to talk about and delineate one women's journey with masturbation.

"Linda Troeller embodies Maria's experience within this sexually evocative photograph, which was chosen as a judges favorite in the 'Women's Erotic Art Exhibition 2014'. She has captured Maria's sensual feeling of paintbrushes on her body as she creates her own unique journey to Orgasm. The shot is close-up filling the whole of one's field of view; so much so that Maria's head disappears above us. This leaves us with the feeling that we are almost there sharing Maria's experience.

This image is part of a series of photographs and interviews undertaken with the ethnographer Marion Schneider entitled Orgasm: involving women of different ages, nationalities, cultural and sexual backgrounds.

I was touched by Linda's sensitive way of working with these women, accomplished in the approach that she used to gain their trust and confidence before being photographed: for example, she used the experience of shopping with Maria as a fait accompli before the photographic shoot. I believe it is this down-to-earth approach that set the scene for Maria to pose in such an empowering and celebratory way.

As a Psychotherapist I understand the experience of Orgasm as one where we are in absolute contact with ourselves; a place where our internal mind simultaneously links to the here-and-now physical bodily feeling; resulting in completeness within oneself.

Linda breaks all the taboos around sexuality that should never have been there in the first place; she puts women back in the driving seat."

Helene Williams is a practicing Art Psychotherapist in addition to being an artist. www.helenewilliams.com ‡

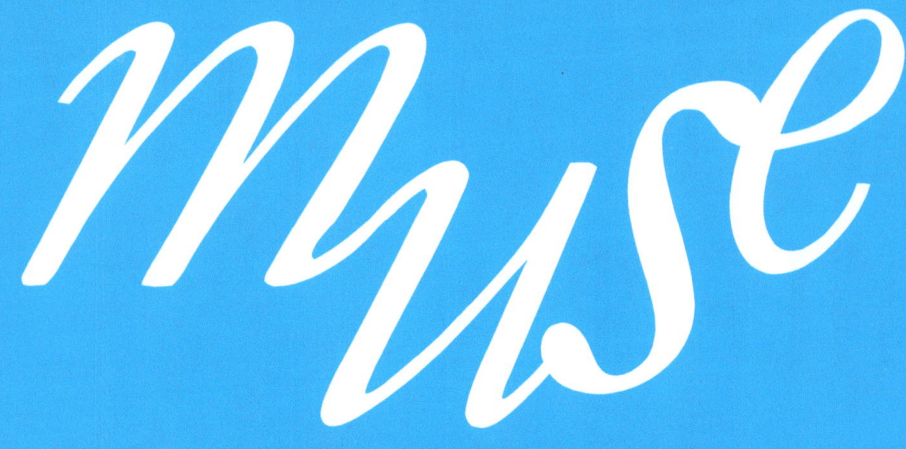

In front of the lens

Model Name: *Anoush Anou*
Location: *Columbus, OH*
Years Modeling: *5*
Style of modeling: *Fine art & fashion-nudes*

What brought you to modeling?

Before I modeled for photographs, I modeled for artists/painters, a job which initially appealed to me due to its flexible hours and creative environment. I did this for two years, full-time and just through people I met at art classes or by word of mouth. I would occasionally get asked to model for a photographer. Eventually I decided to transition to photographic modeling completely and I've never looked back!

What are the top things that have helped you become a successful model?

I think that professionalism plays an enormous role in keeping my calendar full. I work really hard to return emails as quickly as I can (although still not as fast as I'd like to) and to communicate details clearly and concisely. I turn up to shoots on time, fed, slept and organized. I've had many photographers comment on this so I feel like it goes a long way with them.

Aside from that I think that good body-awareness, emotiveness and creativity are what makes any model a great model.

What was the toughest assignment you've had?

There is not one experience which stands out as being particularly bad, and I've been very lucky with the photographers with whom I've worked so if anything has gone wrong, it's rarely had anything to do with them. The most difficult assignments I've had have mostly been due to unfavorable weather conditions. Working outside when it's insanely hot or cold can be very painful. I try to be smart about this and I won't book outdoor nude shoots when it's obviously the wrong season for it, but you can't always depend on the weather report and I've definitely been caught out more than a few times!

What is the hardest lesson modeling has taught you?

I think that one of the biggest challenges, and certainly one of the things which I'm most grateful for the opportunity to practice, has been in learning to appreciate what I am bringing to the table as a creative. I find it so easy to see what makes the artists who I admire so compelling, but much harder to see the beauty in my own work.

What have you learned about yourself through modeling?

This is probably an obvious answer but I feel that modeling has made me more comfortable in my own skin. It's very humbling to see yourself, from almost every imaginable angle, in an endless variety of (sometimes

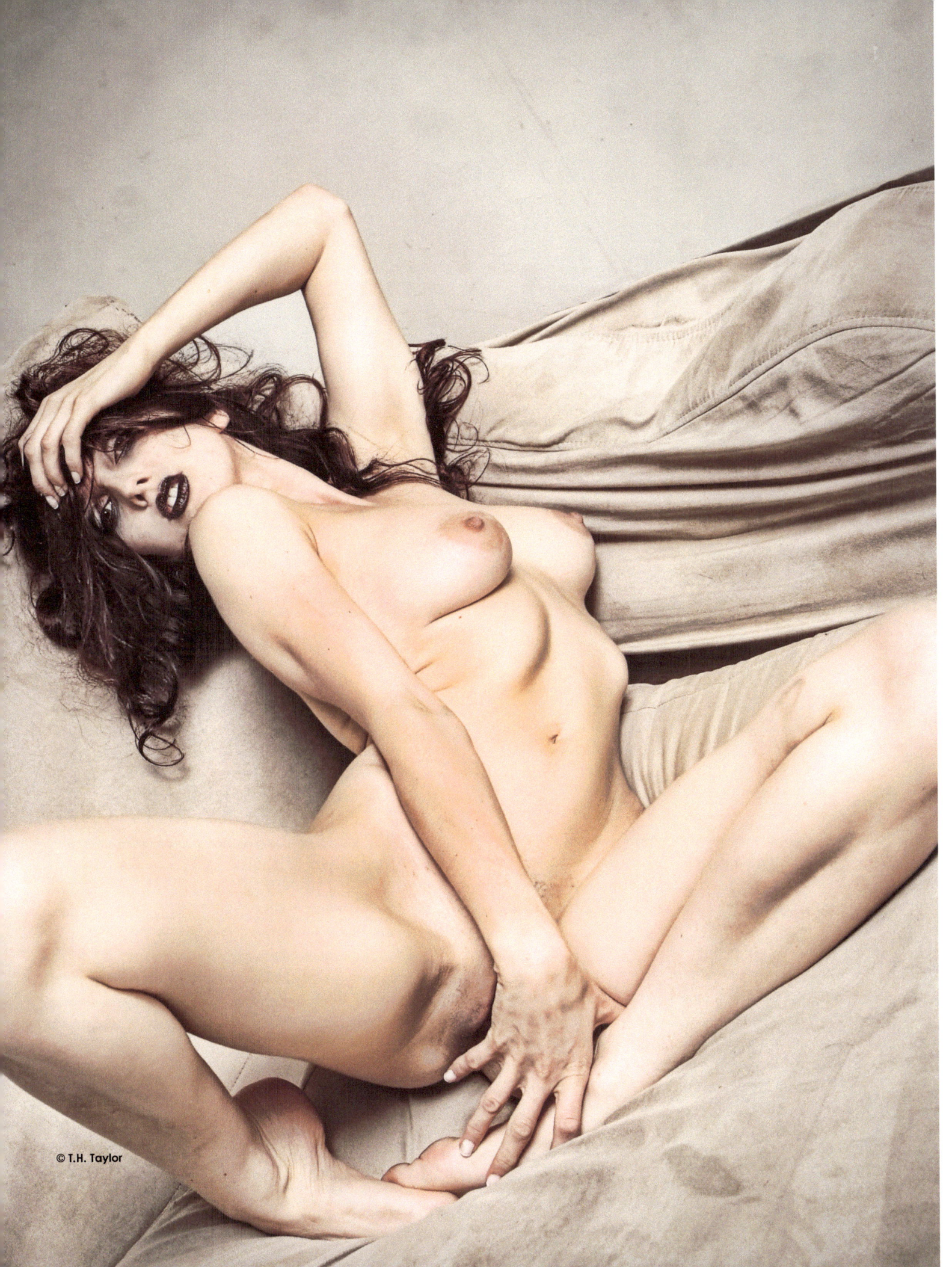

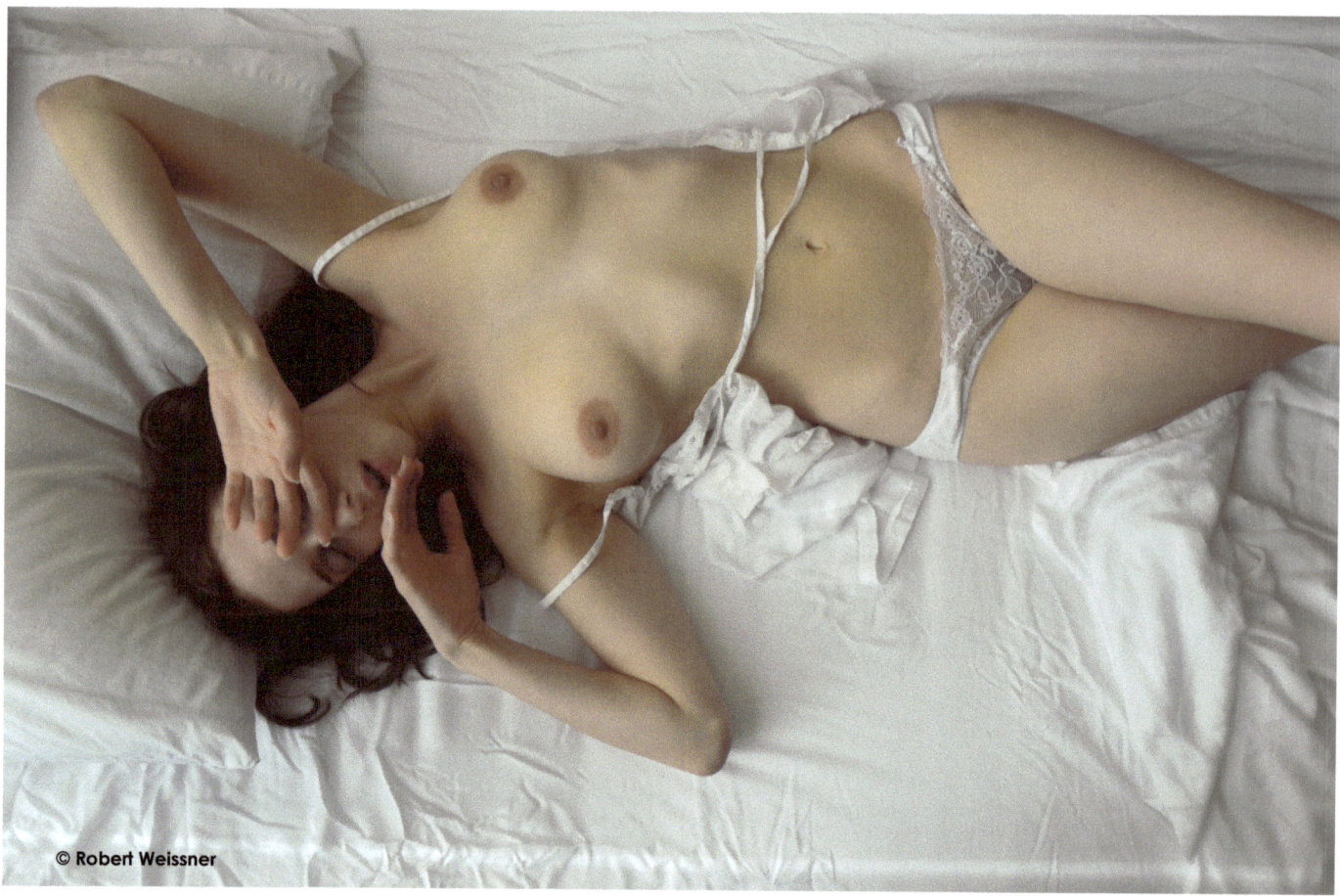

© Robert Weissner

unflattering) lighting conditions. I think it gives you a different sense of yourself.

It has made me realize, too, how open to perception any two dimensional image is. I could look at 10 different photographs of me and see myself look like 10 different people... Yet all of them are accurate. I find that interesting.

What is the most common trait you see in talented photographers?
An understanding that the moment which exists when they click the shutter matters more than their equipment.

One thing that I find challenging as a model is seeing so many potentially wonderful photographers who, in my opinion, over-think the creative process; seeing art as a mathematical equation and overlooking the integrity of the moment they're seeking to capture while they're calculating the answer; believing it needs to be difficult to be good. I'm certain that the moment is

nearly all that matters, if there is nothing real to photograph, then there is nothing.

When I find a photographer who is willing to be unprepared and who can surrender to the scenario, one who understands that window light and a wall is all we need and that it doesn't really matter what, if anything, I'm wearing, well... that's why I do this.

What would be the most important piece of advice you'd give other models?
I think that honing in on what makes you unique will help you get to you where you want to be and will save you a lot of frustration along the way. No one else in the world looks or emotes just the way that you do, so working out how best to celebrate what is really at the core of you is a much better use of energy than trying to replicate another model's work or style. In my own experience, self-exploration is very much synonymous with the type of artistic expression which feels truly meaningful. ‡

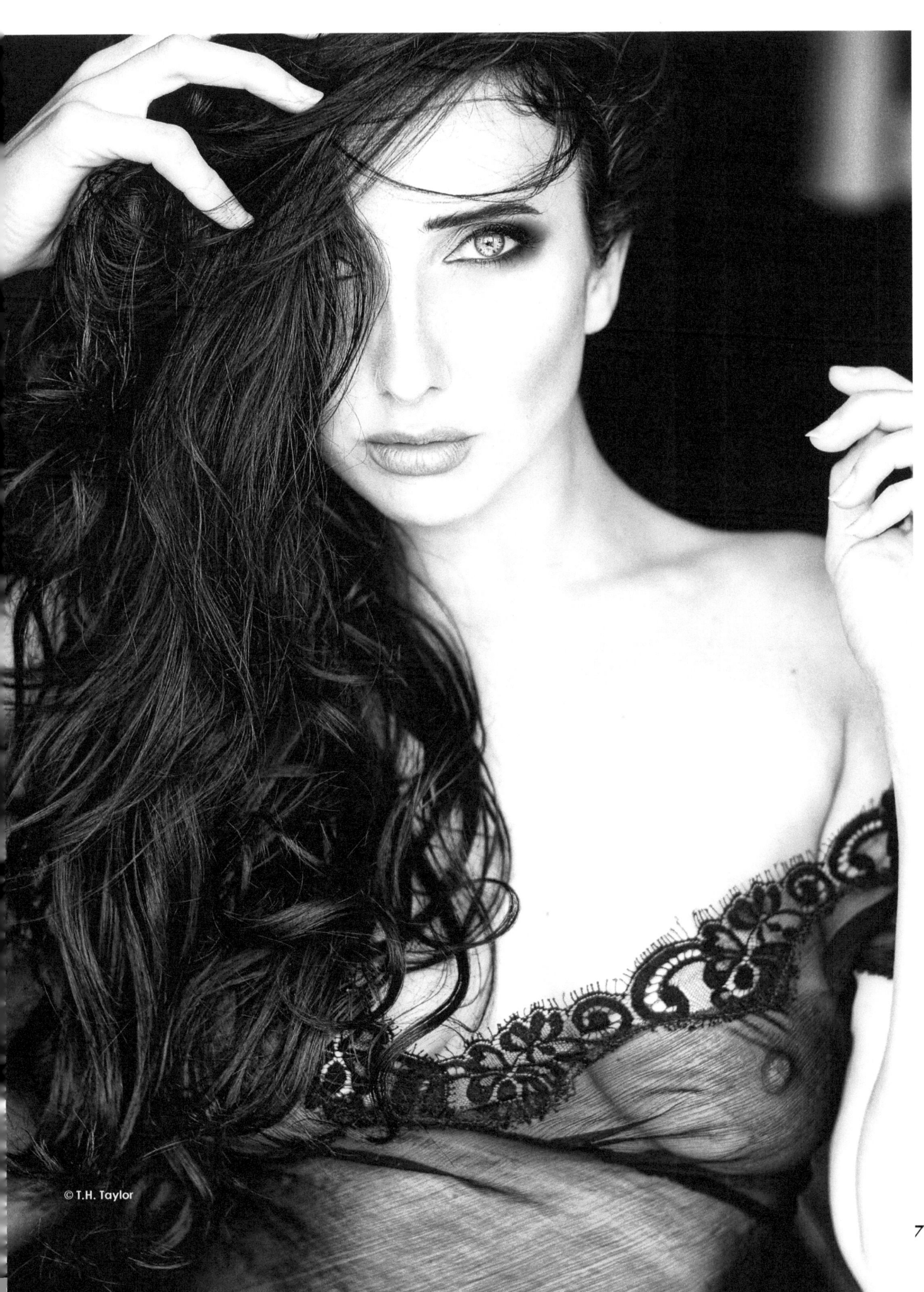

© T.H. Taylor

7

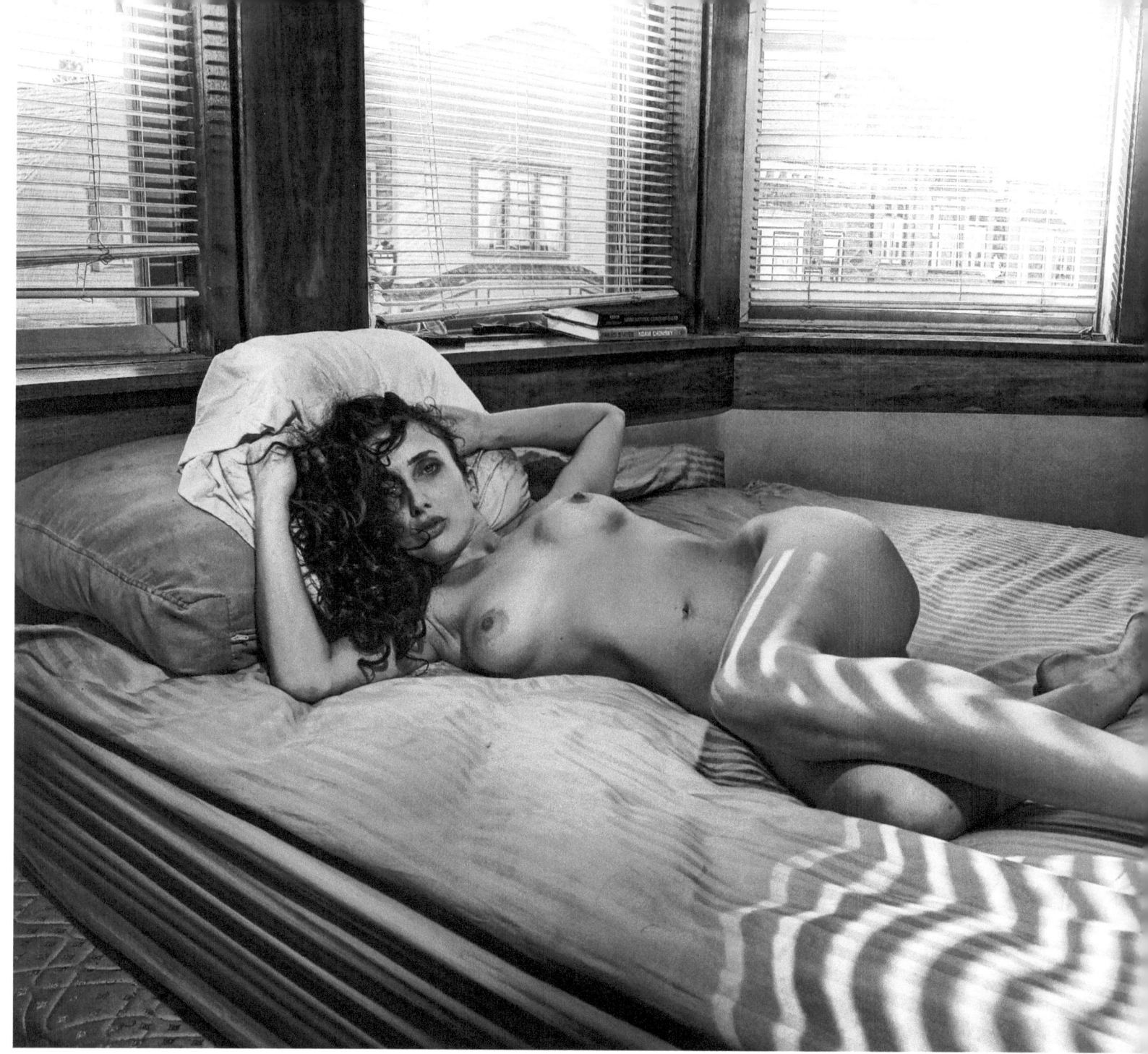

© T.H. Taylor

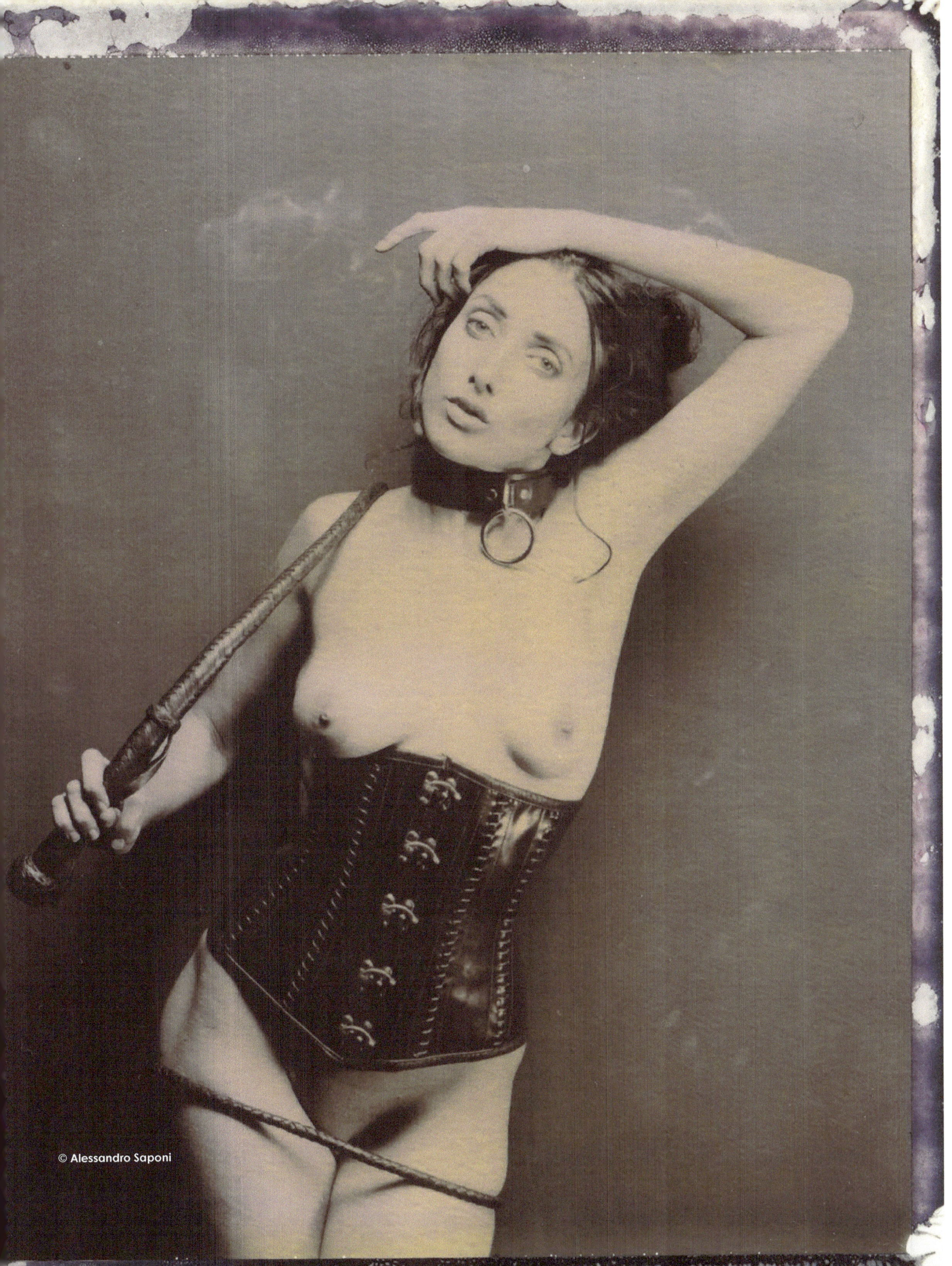

© Alessandro Saponi

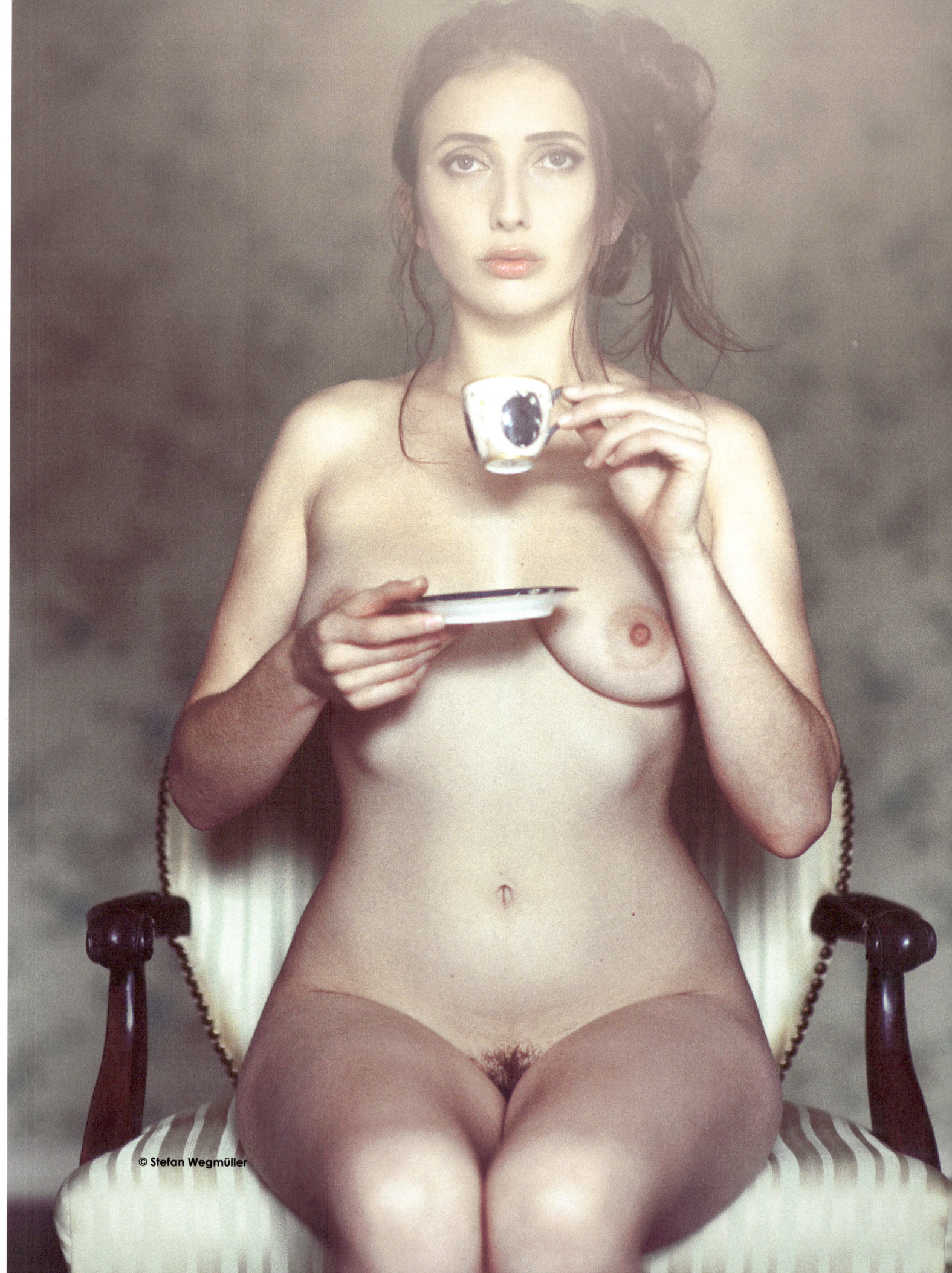

© Stefan Wegmüller

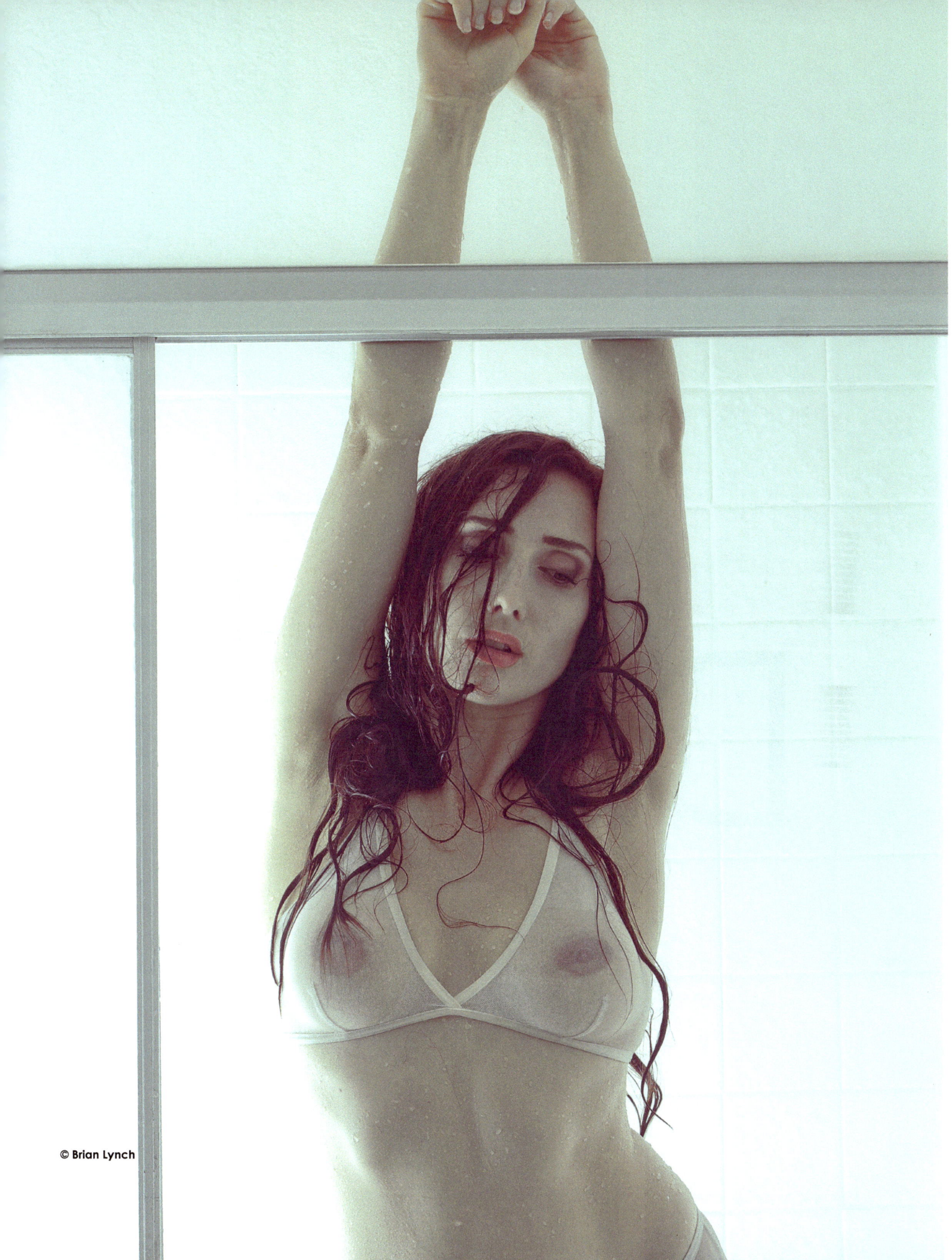

Eli Dijkers

The main subject of my photographic work are humans, often subtracted from their connections. In my photography, I capture the world as I perceive it. A world in which light and darkness co-exist side by side. ‡

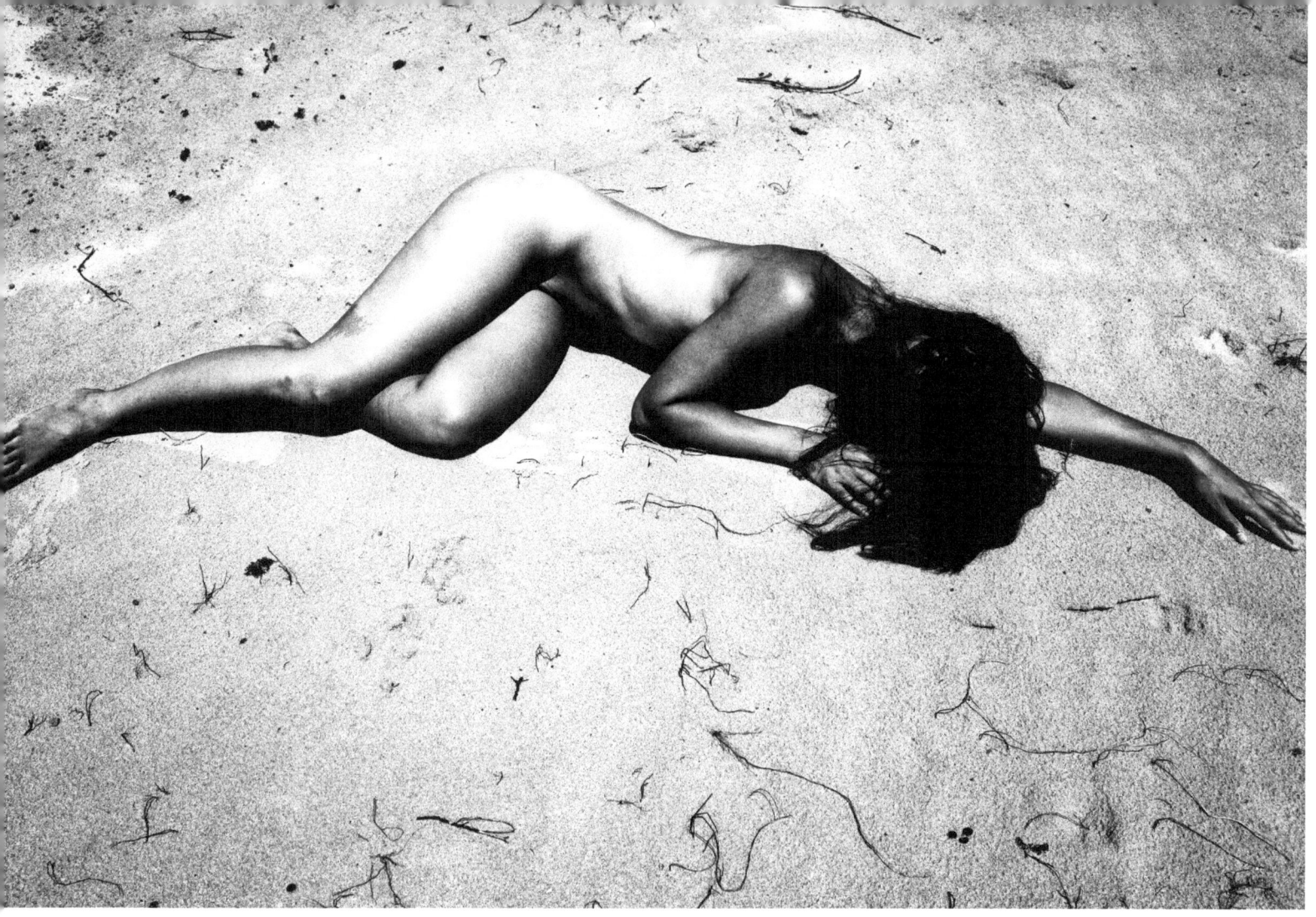

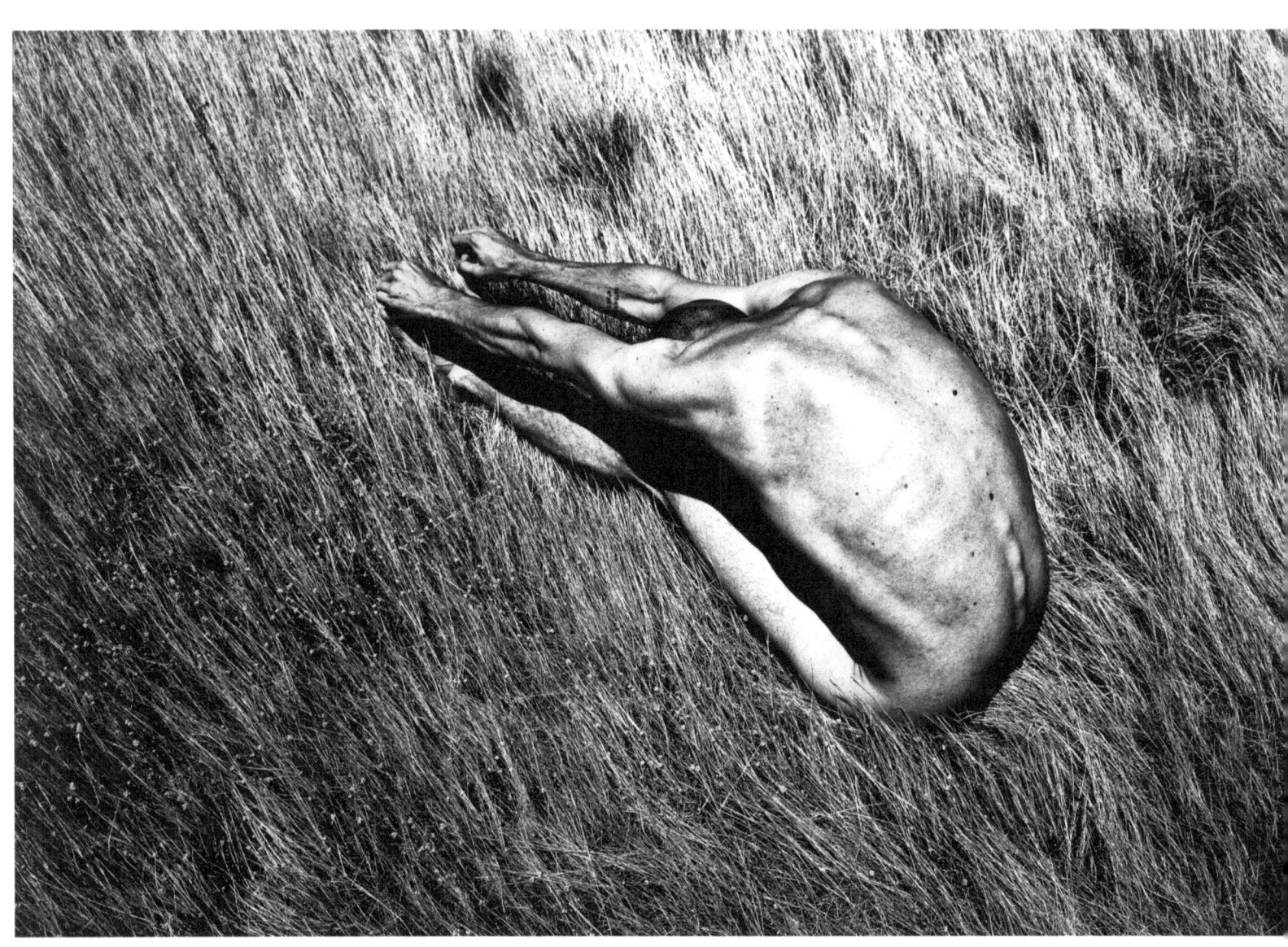

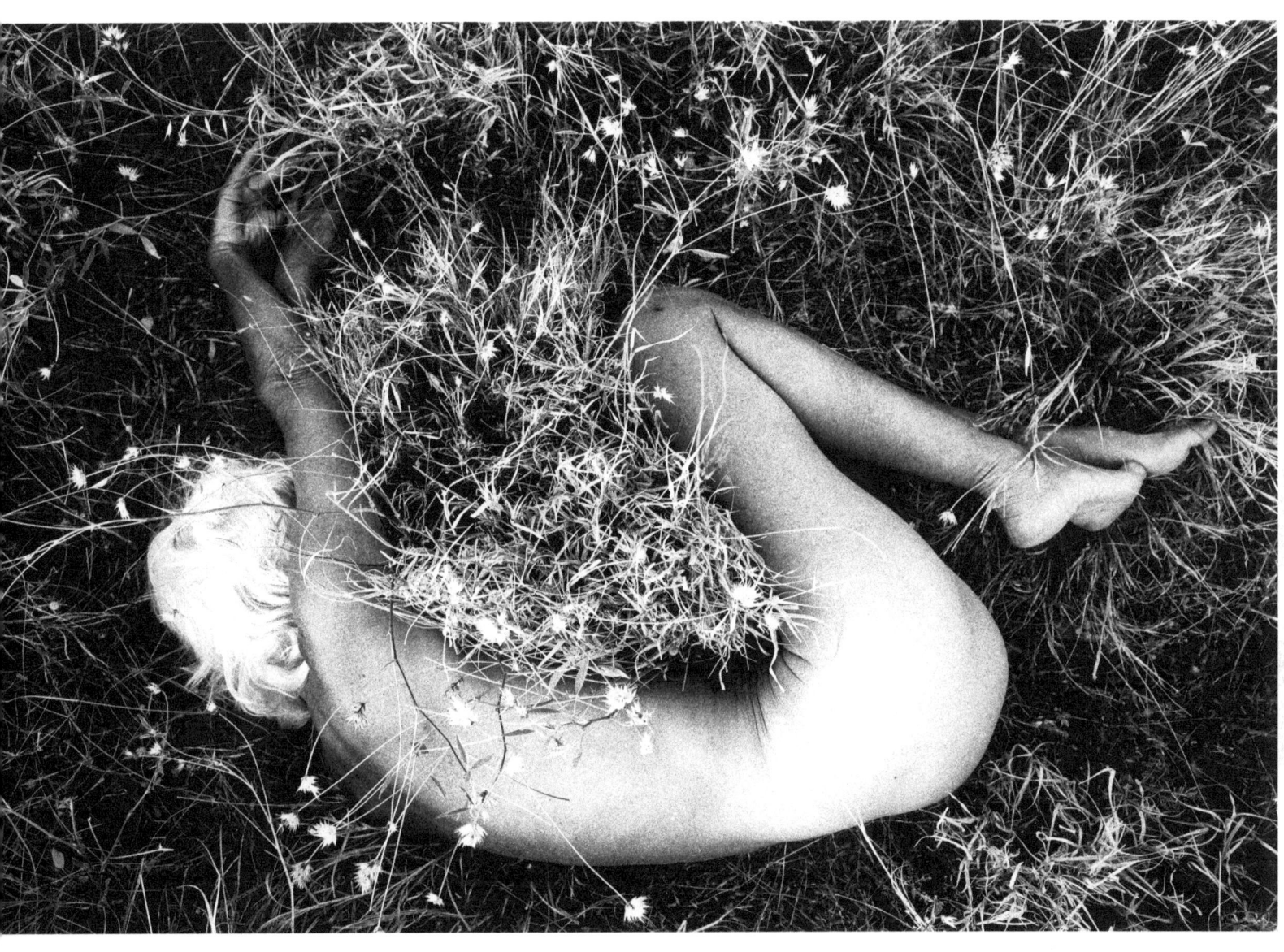

Feliz Paloma Gonzalez

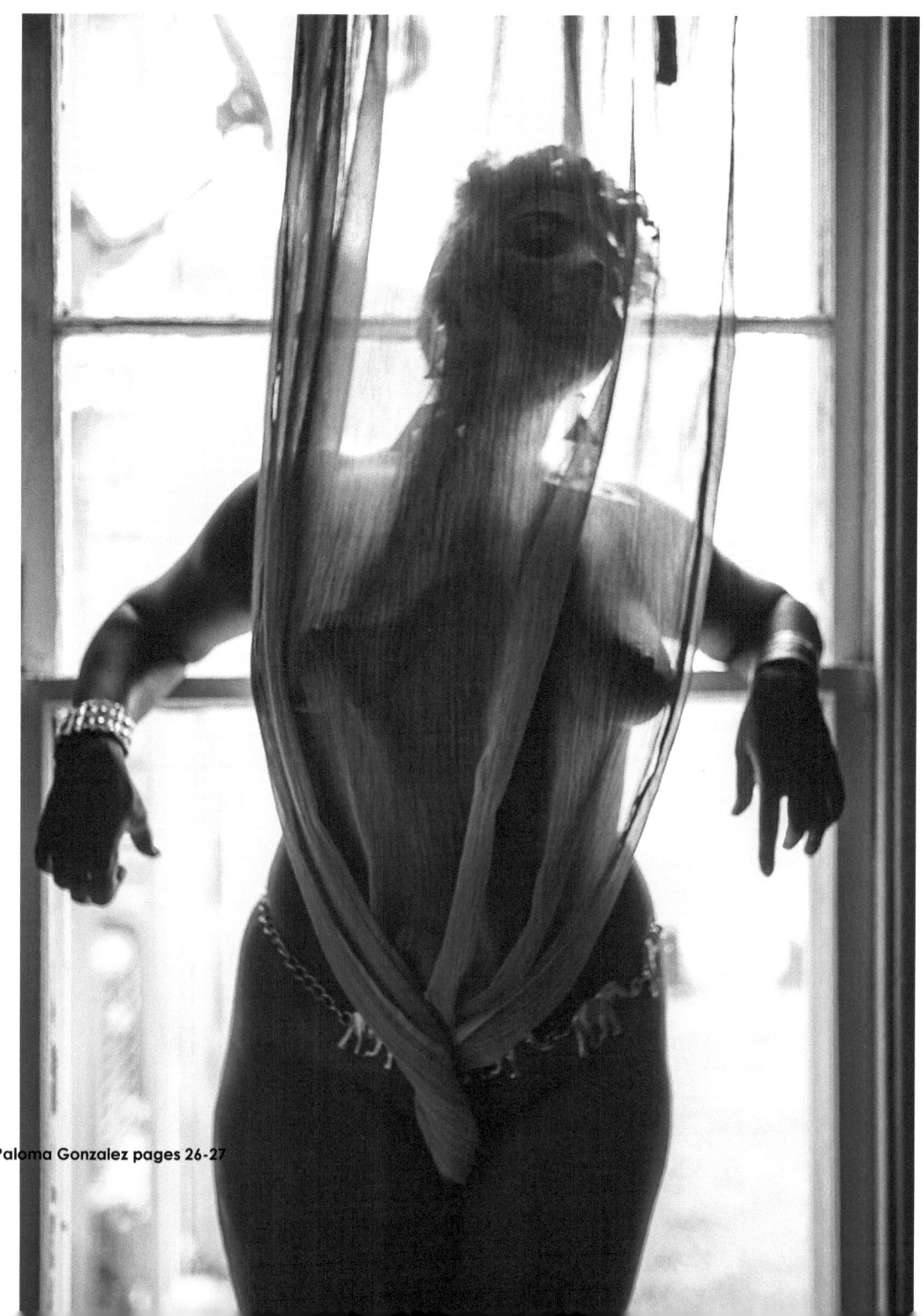

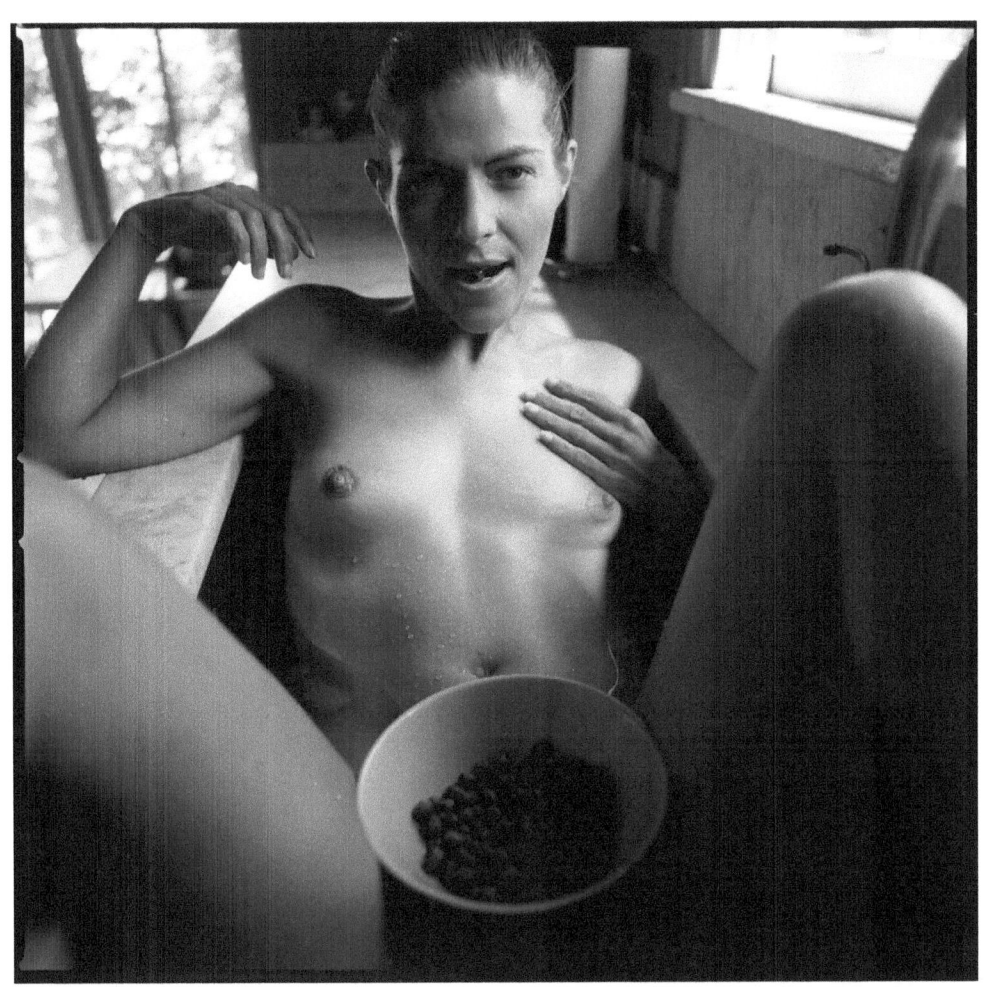

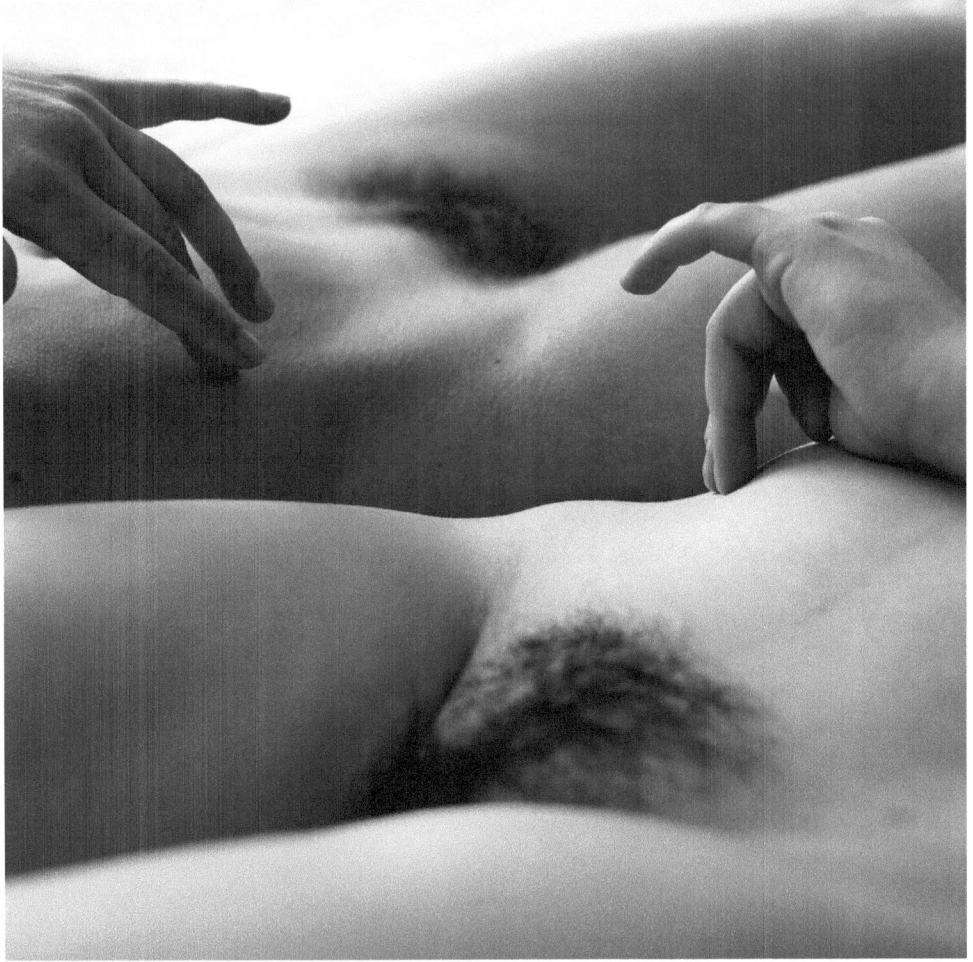

SH SADLER

SH Sadler came into existence as an artistic collaboration between Julia SH and Nic Sadler in 2012. Drawing form a diverse range of skills and influences, our work primarily, though not exclusively, explores the sculptural form of the nude. Recent work includes portraits of Daft Punk for Australian JJJ Magazine and a cover for Icing Magazine, published in February 2015.

Julia was born in Stockholm, Sweden, where she studied theater and performance. In 2002, she moved to London to continue her studies, obtaining her BA in Fine Art (film/video/performance) from Central Saint Martin's College of Art and Design in 2005, and her MFA in Fine Art (media) from the Slade School of Fine Art in 2007. She currently lives in Los Angeles where she works as a film editor and photographer.

Nic was born in the UK, graduating from Curtin University in Perth, Western Australia with a BA in Linguistics and Film Studies in 1985. He began his career as a Cinematographer in London in 1995, working on numerous music videos, commercials and feature films. Nic moved to Los Angeles in 2005 where he still lives and works in a variety of disciplines from photography to film-making and software & product design.

Our goal is to create dramatic images that force the viewer to re-evaluate the concept of beauty and challenge the prevailing aesthetic. ‡

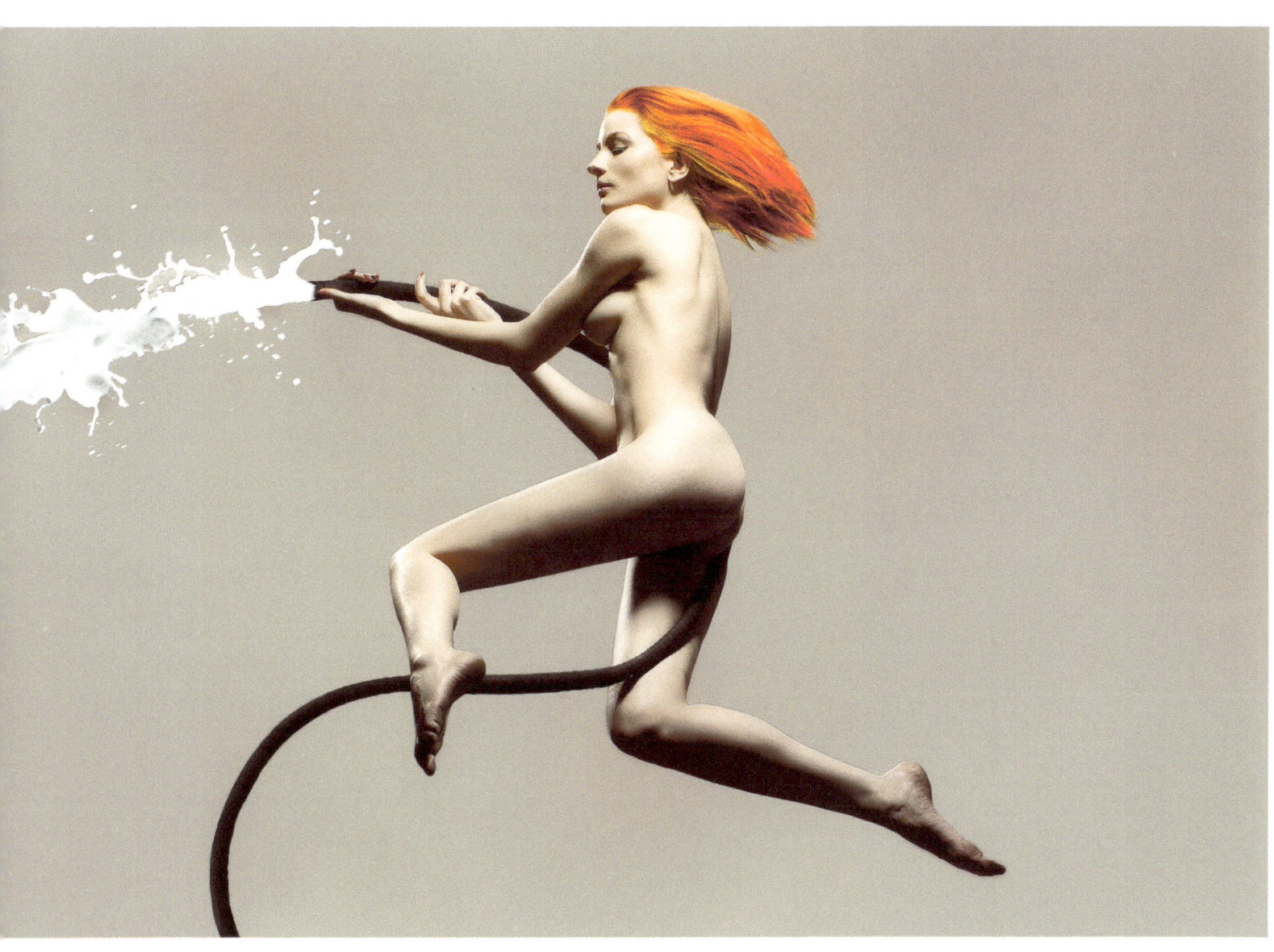

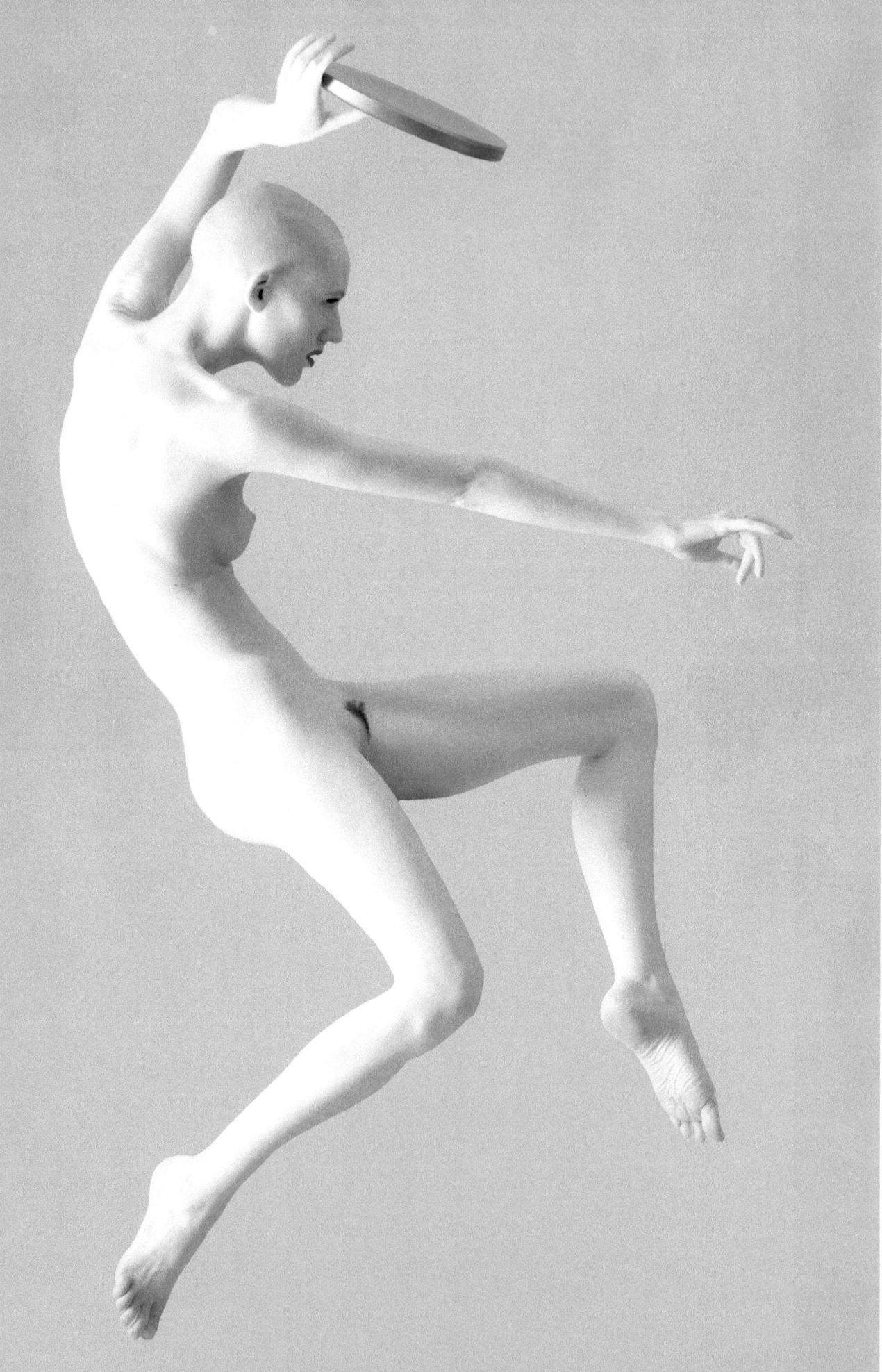

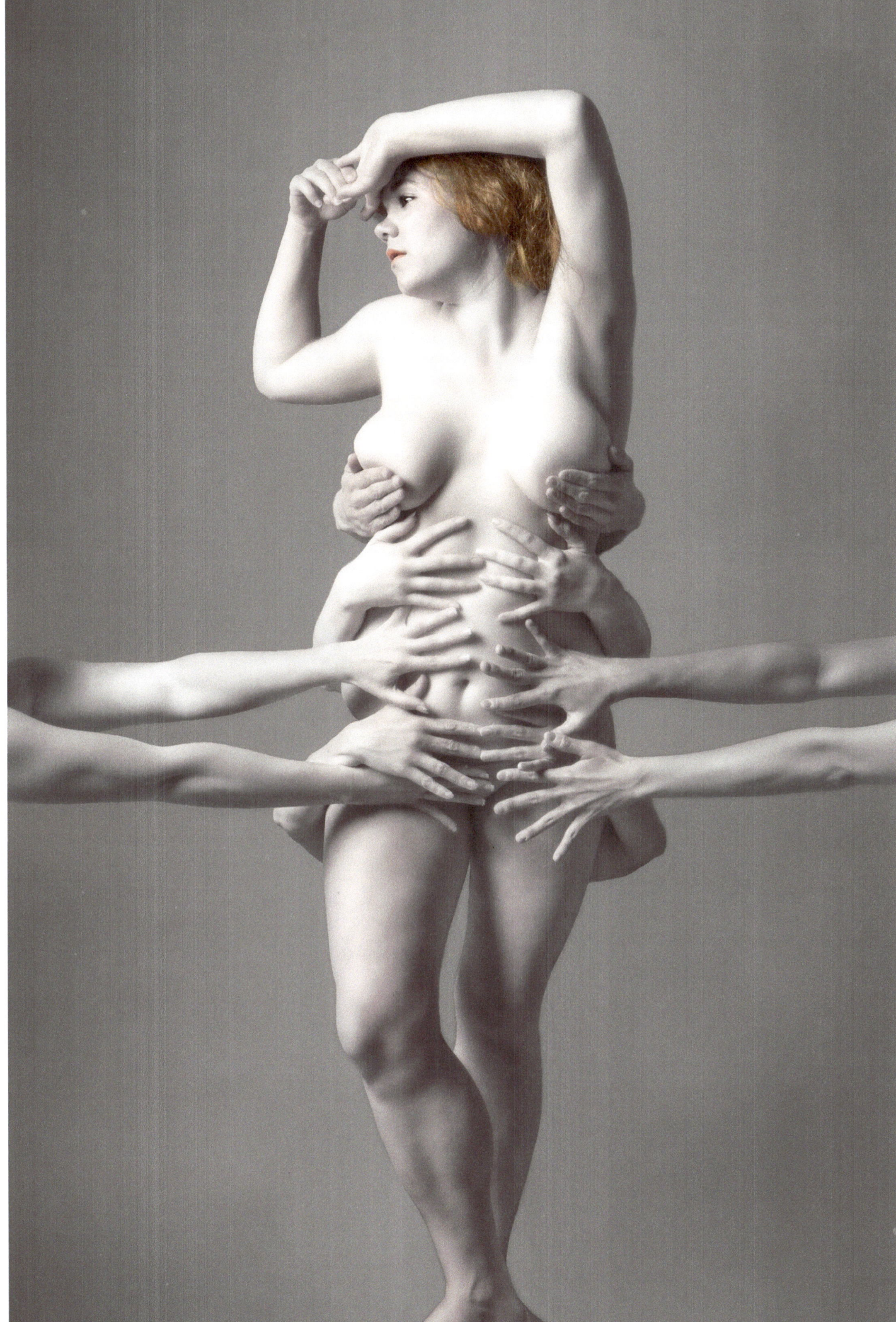

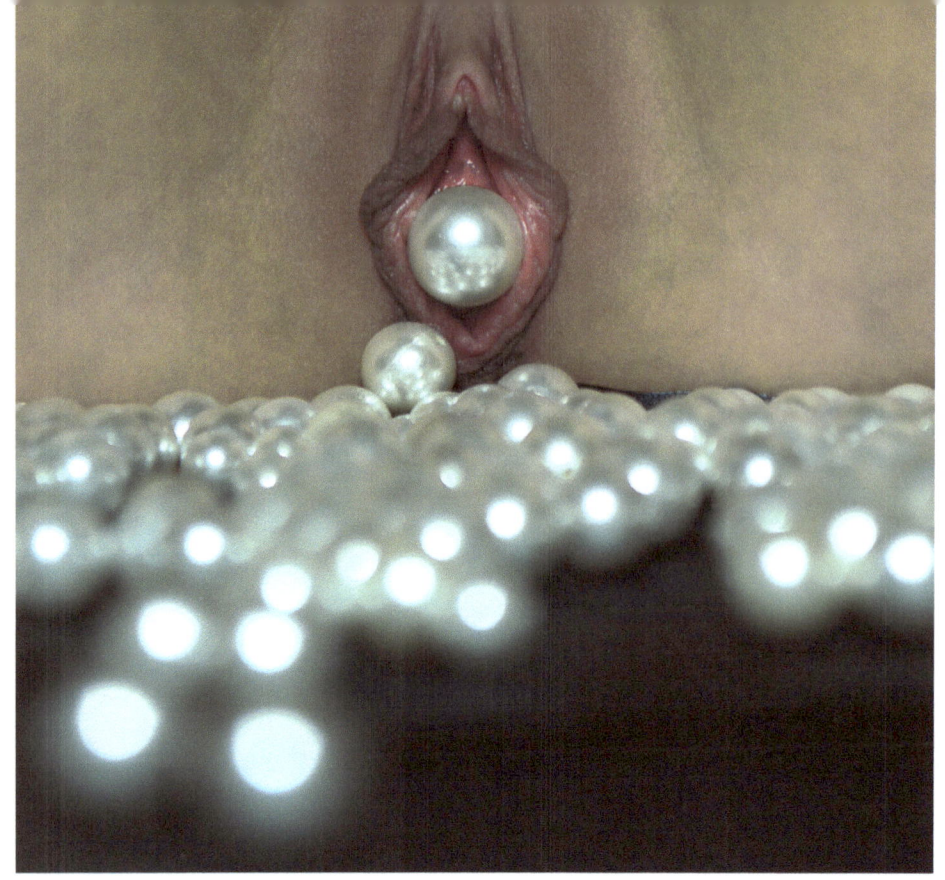

K.D. Dickson

My art is for those who view the female form as it should be viewed…as a work of art. There is absolutely nothing more beautiful, artistic, fascinating than the nude female. Nude models are some of the most amazing people and I highly value their trust in me.

I wouldn't consider myself a photographer; I'm an artist with a camera. I have always created art in one form or another. Photography is my current preferred medium. My original intention was to get reference photos for my art and when I viewed my first photo shoot, I realized that the photos were art in and of themselves.

My goal during a photo shoot is to capture the female nude as you have never seen before or at least better than what you have ever seen. But of course all art is very subjective. I will only shoot the female nude. My camera has seen nothing butt. No spelling error, I'm better known as Nothing Butt Naked.

The best compliment I have received for my art was from a heterosexual female upon viewing one of my pieces: "Jeez, that picture makes me horny."

All of the credit goes to the models. Without them, I have no art.

> (Image) Pearls – Model: M.J. Joyce
> (Image) Another Shade of Gray –
> Model: Sieana Brown

My favorite quote is, "Art should disturb the comfortable and comfort the disturbed." The second part works so wonderfully for me. ‡

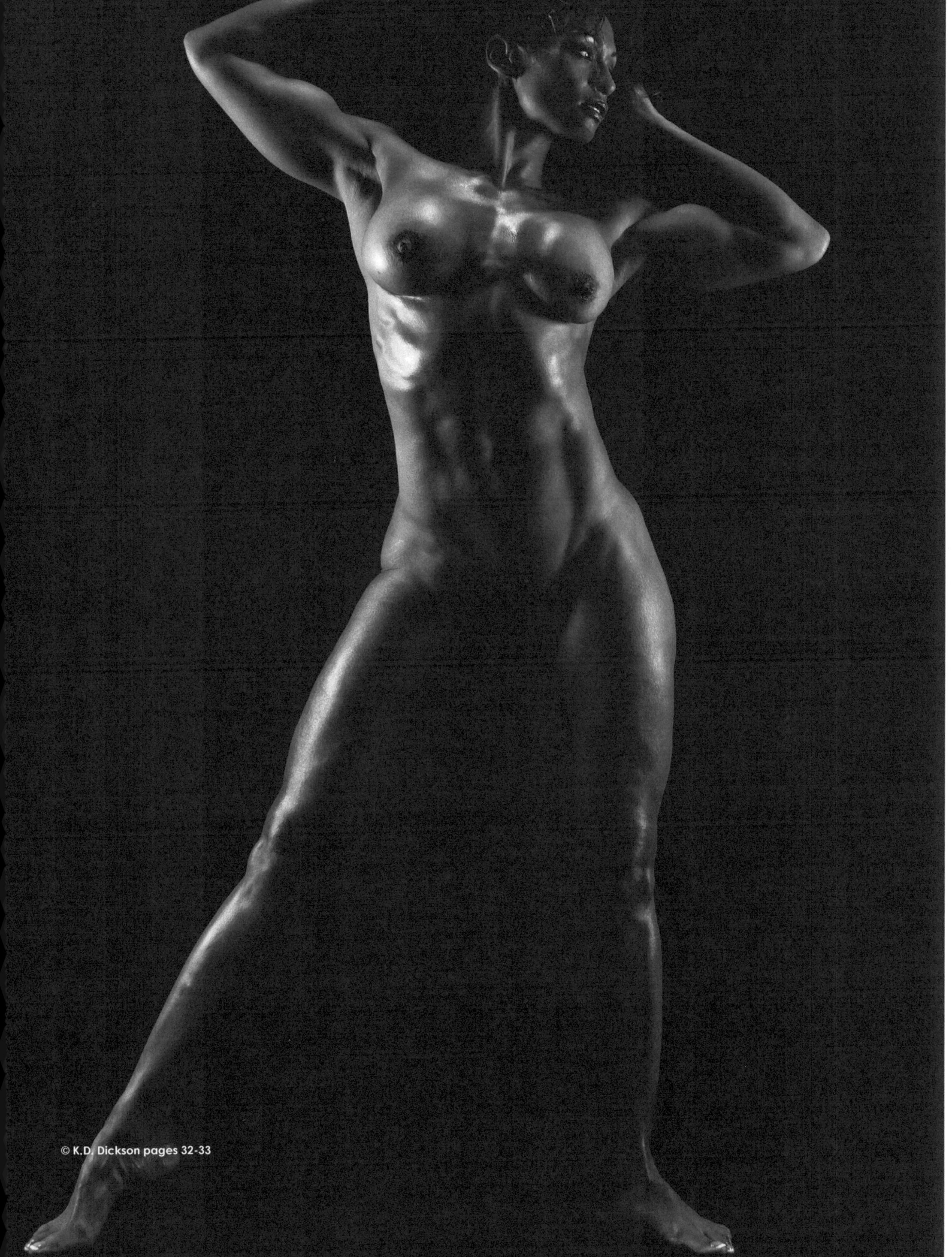

FLORENT BARNADES

I'm a self-taught photographer who's shot for 15 years.
My purpose is to search the simplicity in beauty

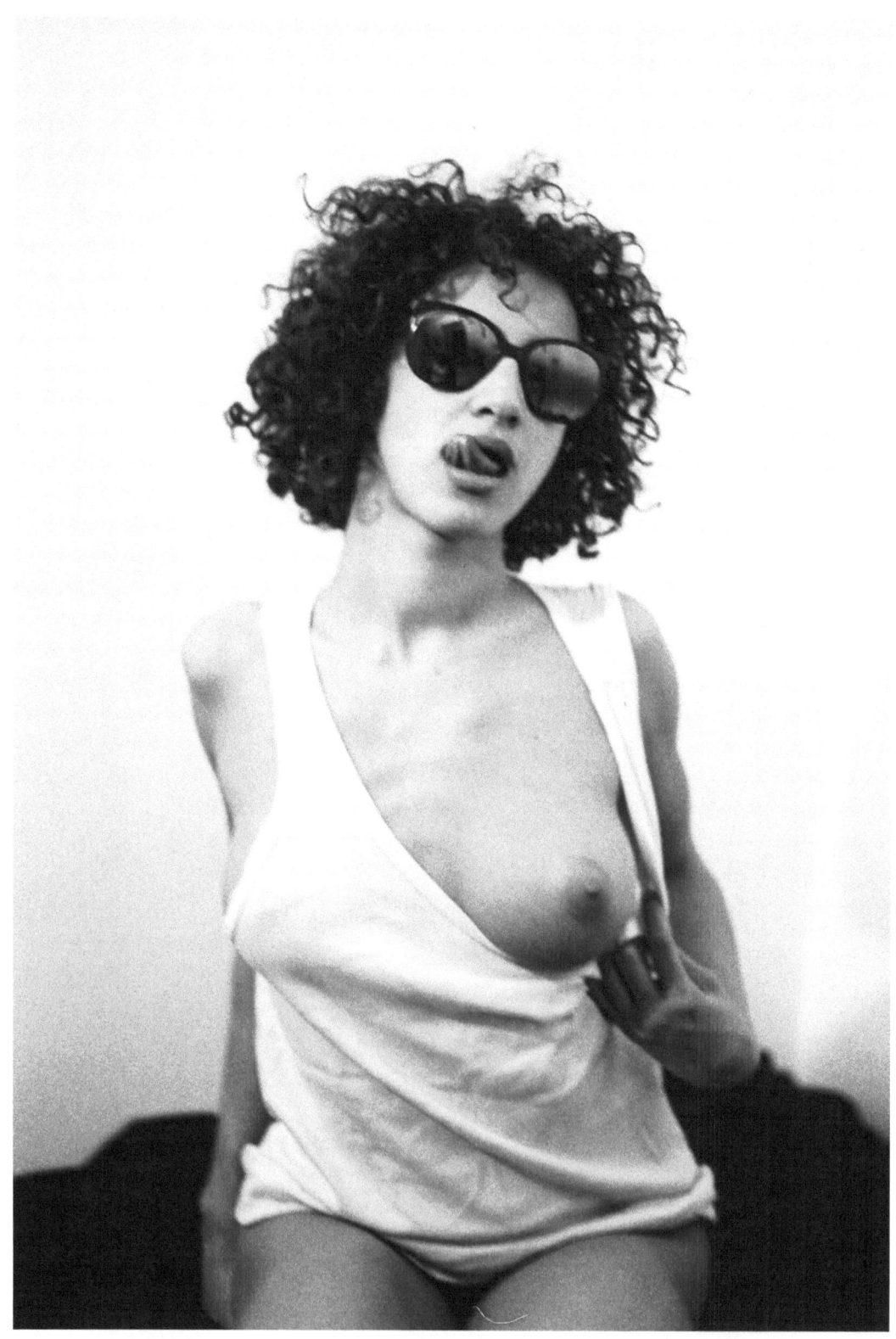

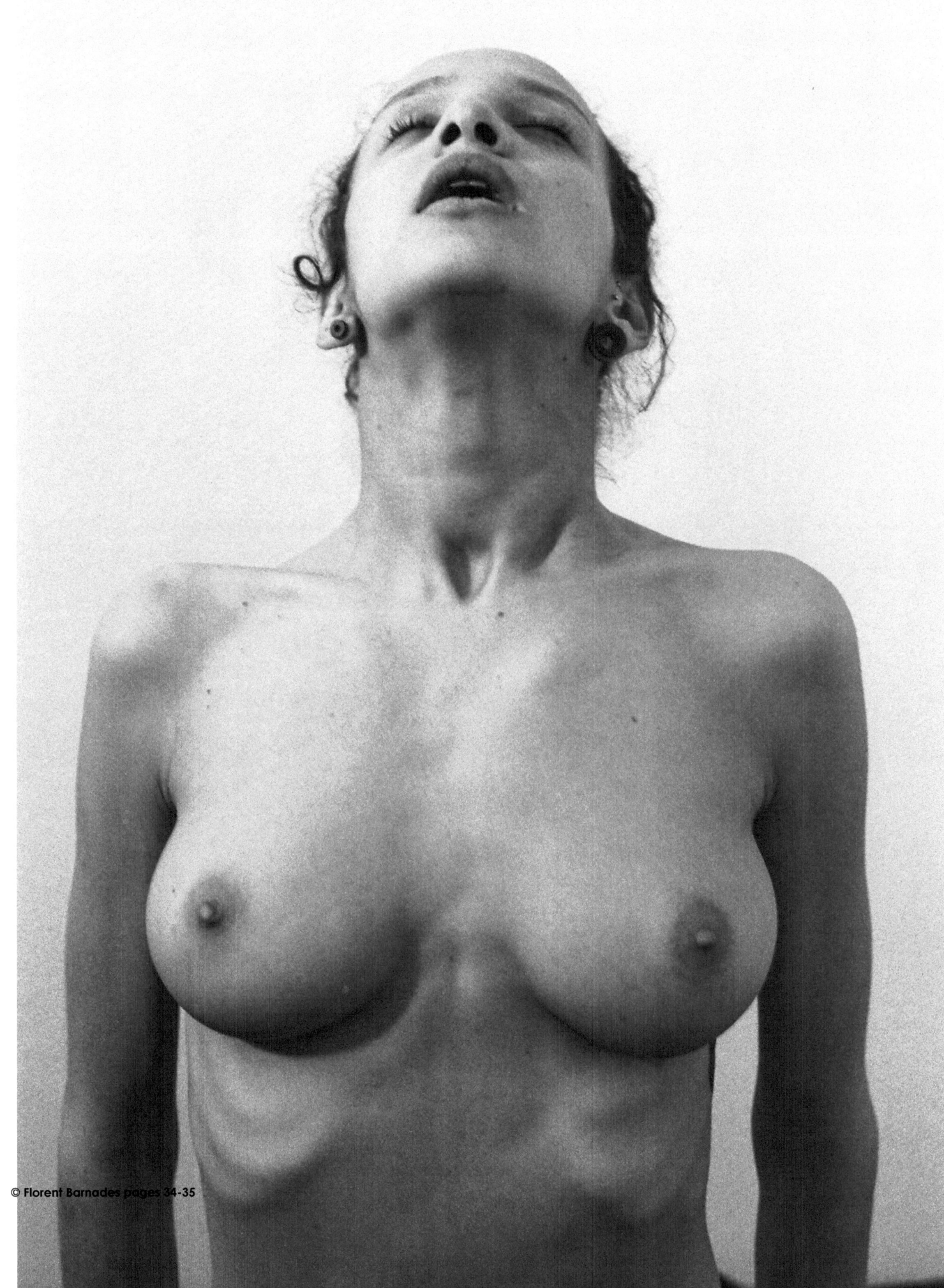

ASP
Photography

I typically prefer to be credited as asp photos, just to maintain some anonymity. My full name is Alan Smith, though, if that makes more sense for the publication.

As for a bio, I originally pursued a career as an illustrator but put down my pencils and brushes in the late '90s and started working at an internet company (like so many others). I came back to art through photography in around 2009. For the past several years, film photography, shooting mostly female subjects in natural light and settings, has dominated my work.

In a moment of stoned epiphany I realized that I wanted to make pictures that look like Marc Bolan songs sound. I reckon that's still a worthy goal. ‡

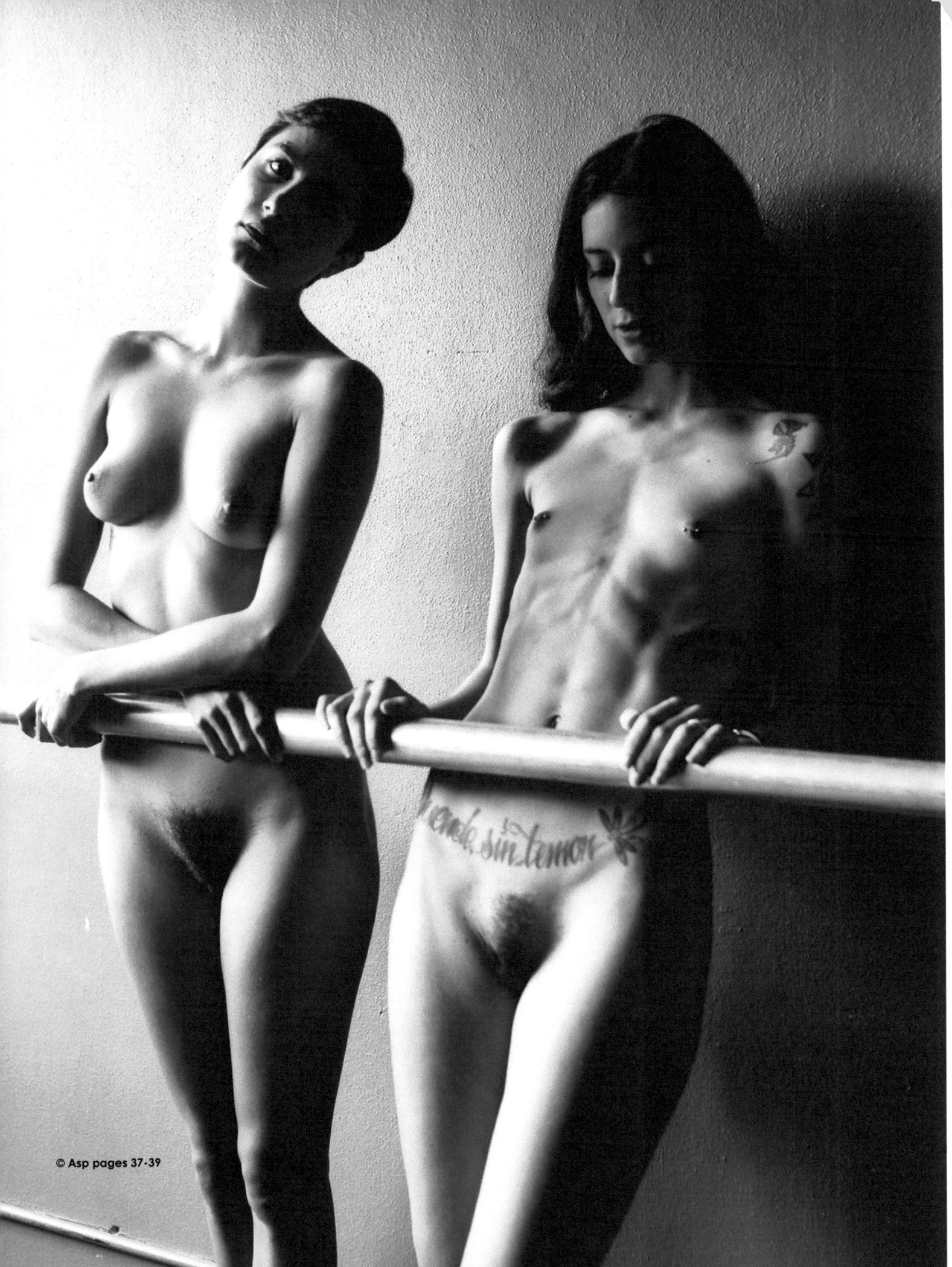

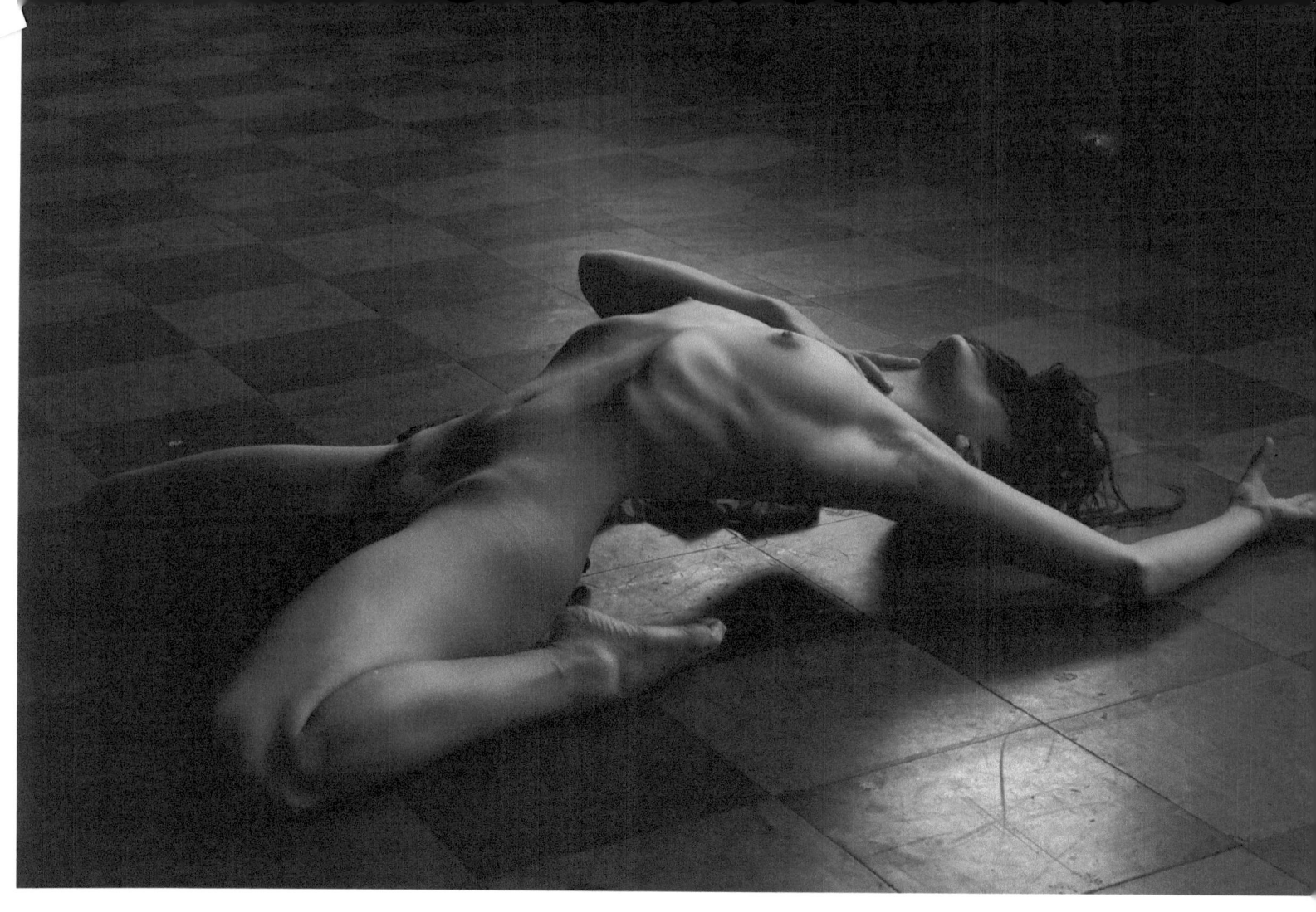

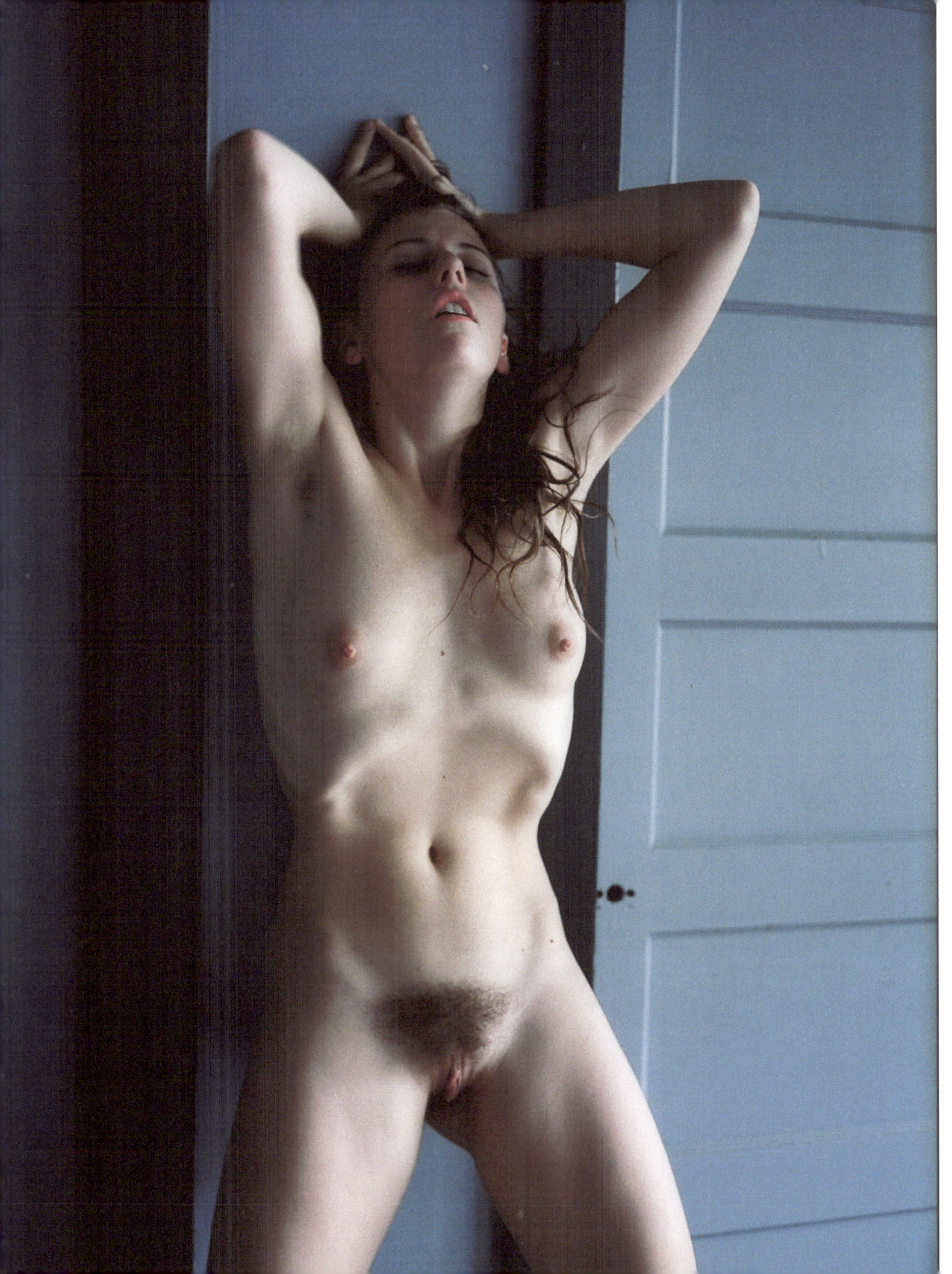

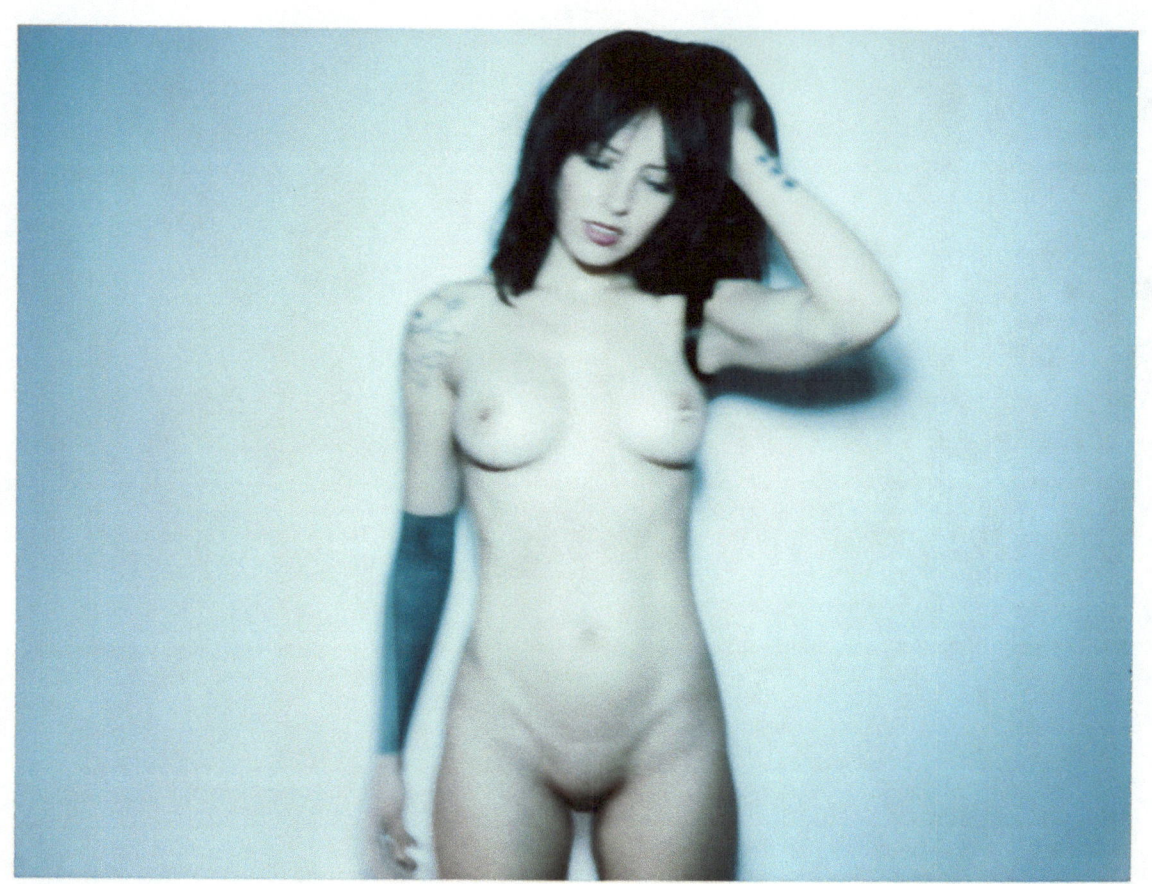

Patrick Cockpit

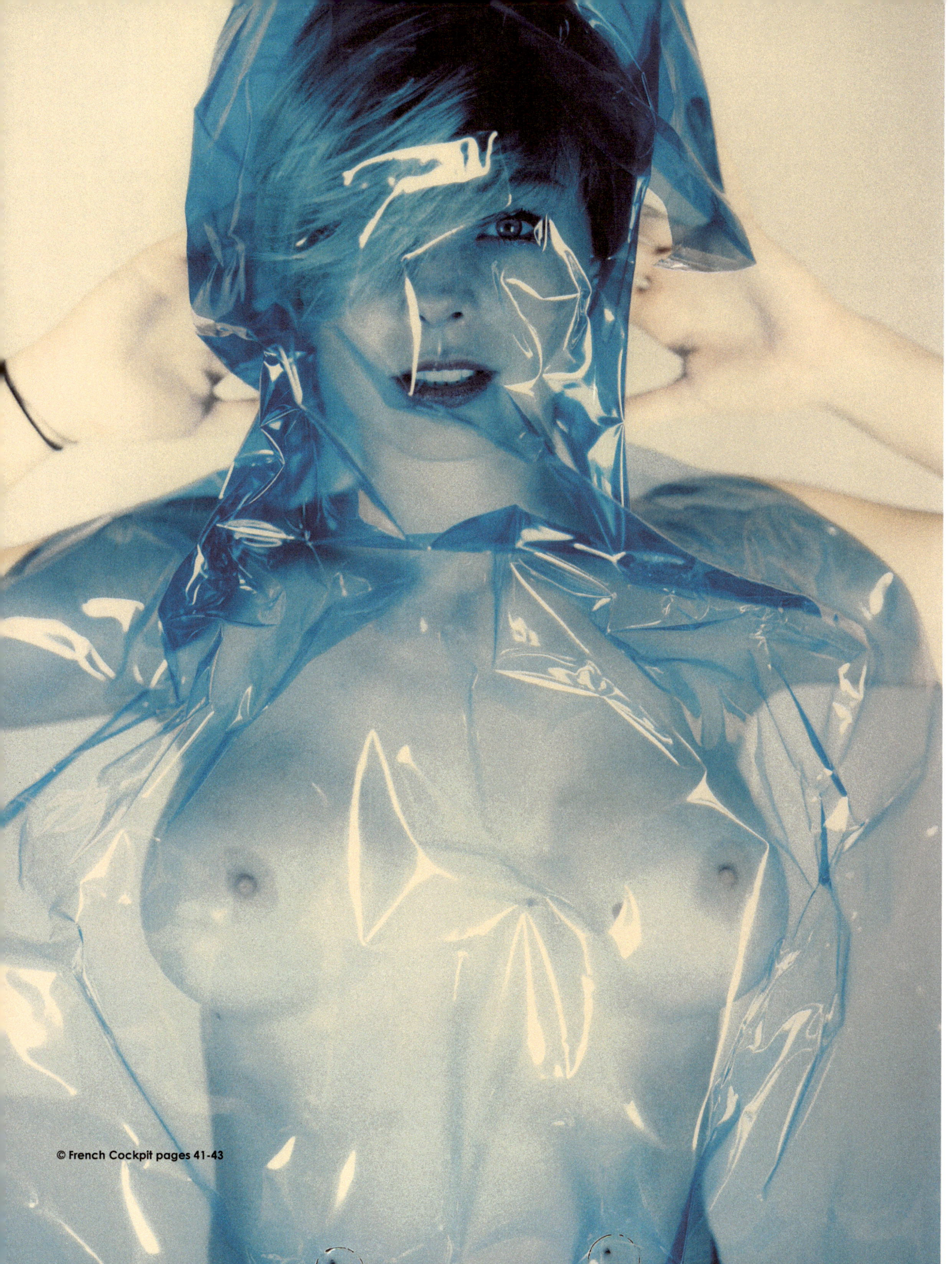

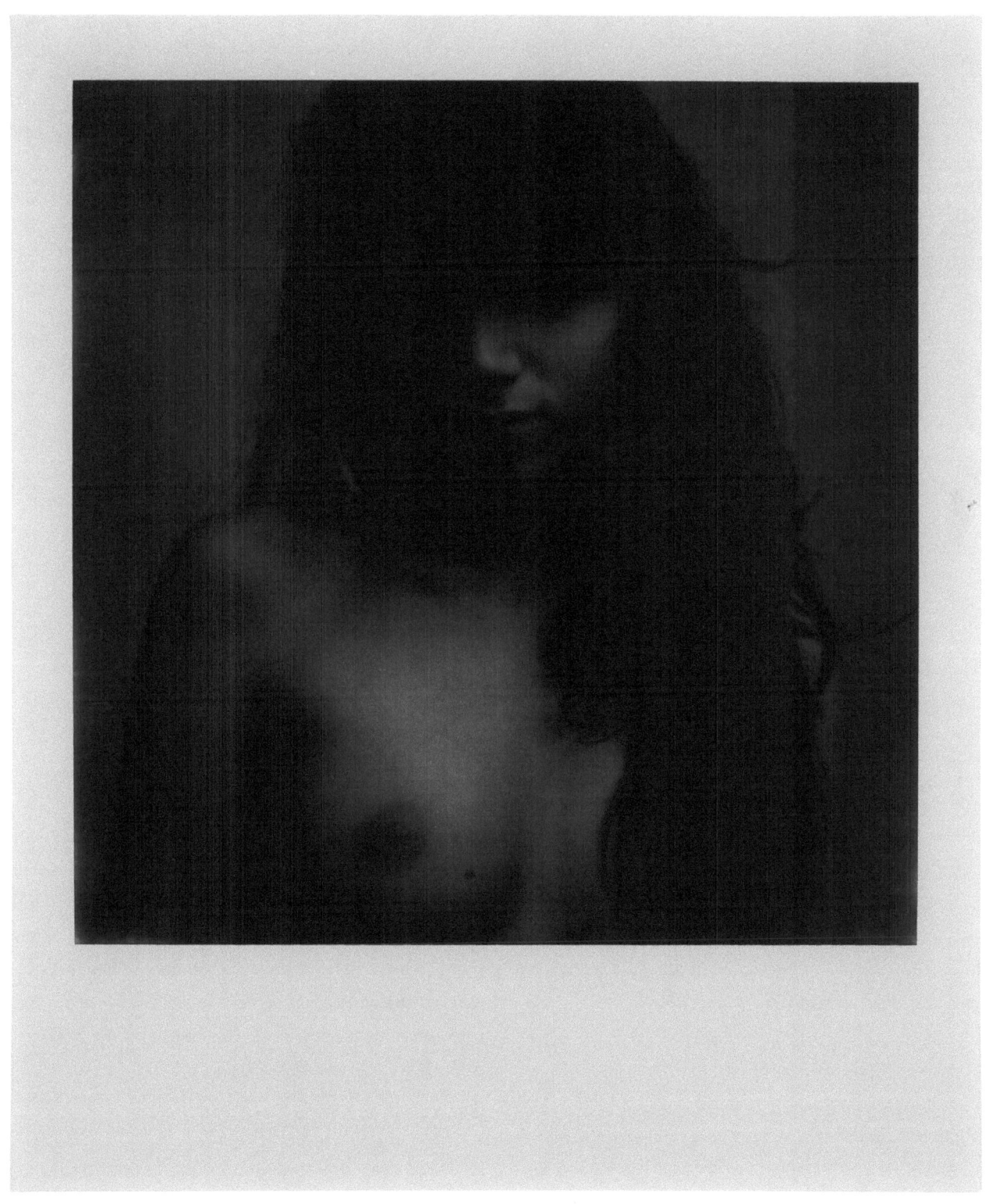

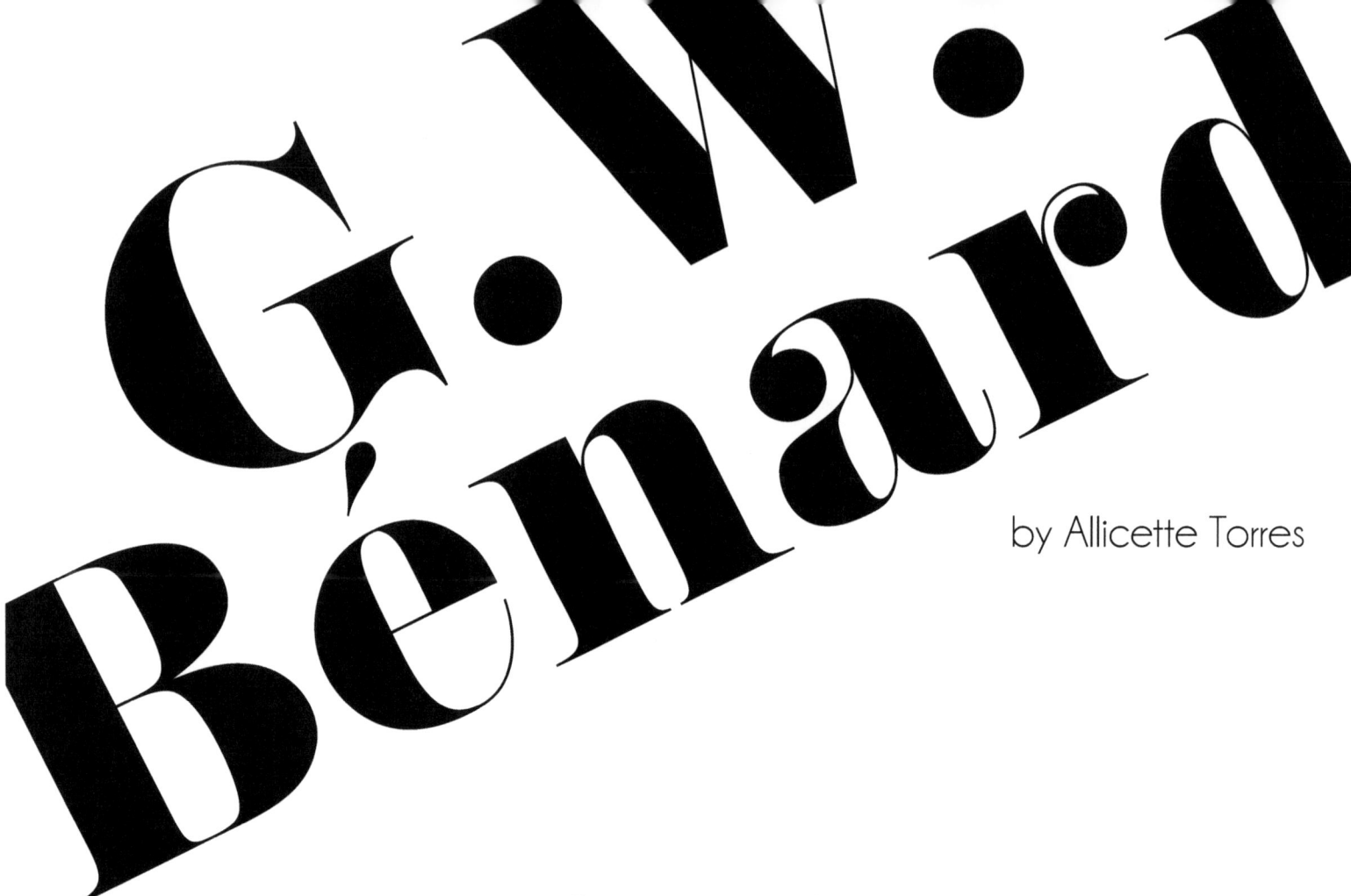

G. W. Bénard

by Allicette Torres

Allicette Torres: Where are you based?
G.W. Benard: I've been living between Lisbon, Barcelona, and Paris.

AT: How long have you been shooting photographs?
G.W.B: I started when I was around 13, but then I took some time without shooting to come back to it again recently. Meanwhile, I had painting and drawing as my mainway of expressing. My drawings were also often nudes. For the last 10 years, photography has been my main way of expressing, parallel to writing.

AT: How did you get started in photography?
G.W.B: I started by doing a course of photography, analogue and dark room, when I was around 13. I wanted to learn it all, the whole process was fascinating. Like magic. The process is also silent, which was something I needed, so maybe it was an excuse to access solitude as well.

AT: What are your go-to cameras now?
G.W.B: I always use an old Asahi Pentax for analogue and Canons for digital.

AT: Film or digital? Why?
G.W.B: It's curious that I started photography through the magic of analogue/darkroom and now I find the magic in digital. It has been more rare for me to shoot in analogue, so nowadays I mostly shoot in digital. It's more "now" and more flexible: being a more flexible tool, digital can give you the analogue approach or the digital one, even when I do the shootings through webcam, like the series "B Shot by a Stranger" about being voyeur of naked loneliness.

AT: What drew you to your particular style?
G.W.B: I always found color, background, and textile to be very distracting; I always preferred them in their own silence. If a ballet dancer is amongst a crowd, it's harder for him to dance; he needs empty space to perform. I like

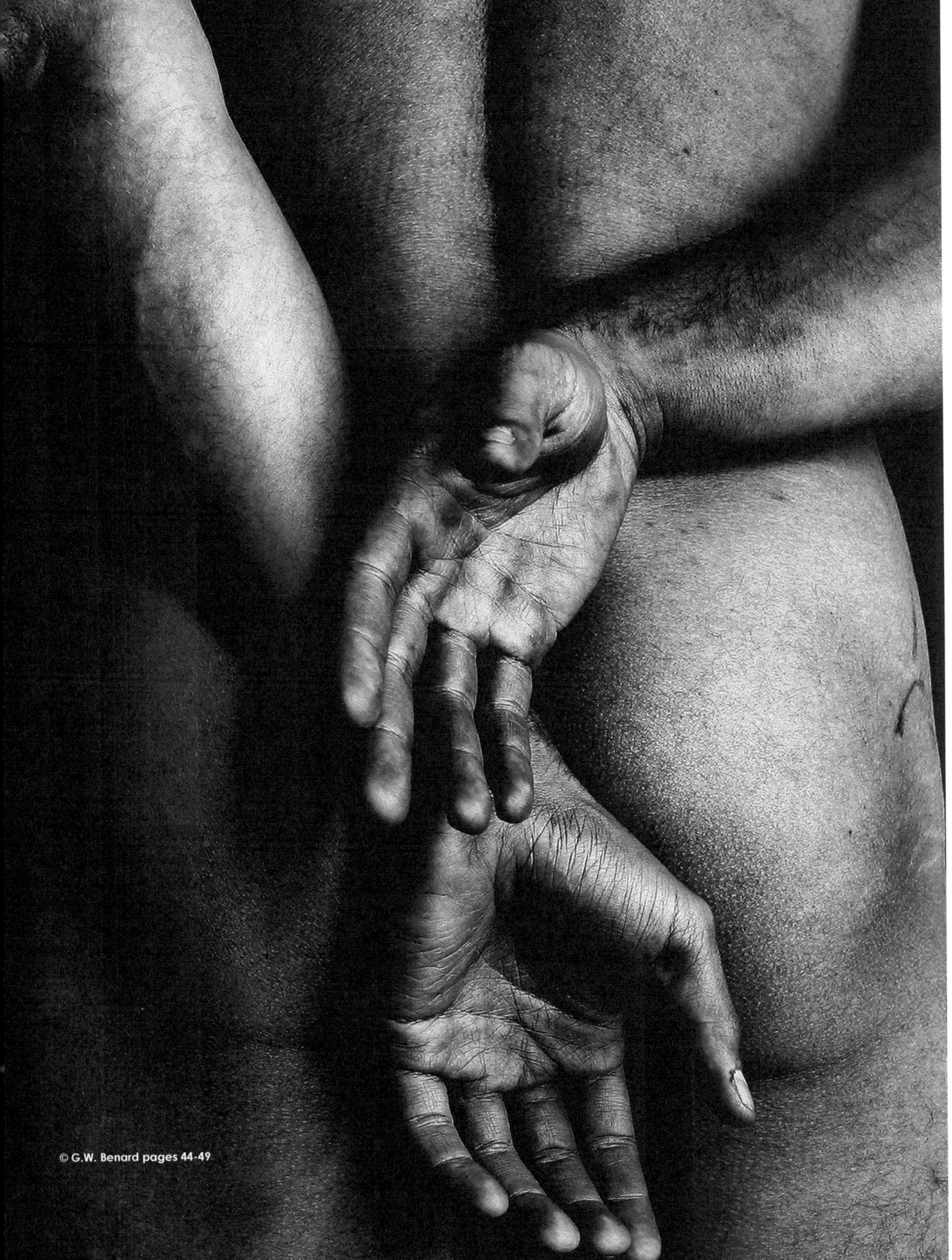

the emptiness around the subject, the work of shadows to bring the light. The non-obvious is to give us space to create. It is the shadow that gives us the concept of light, as it is the emptiness that brings us the form in its pure essence.

AT: What do you want your viewers to take away when they see one of your photographs?

G.W.B: I do photography as a way of expressing myself, but I find my mind silent when I share the final work. Indeed, the work is only fully done when the viewer closes the triangle, traveling through the concept and beyond the aesthetic. There's always much to see beyond the superficial aesthetic, and I often have hidden details in my photographs.

AT: What challenges have you encountered in your work?

G.W.B: Most people engage with a piece of artwork though a fast viewing, which only exposes the obvious.

Also, as an autistic I prefer to go deeper in my silence, so the biggest challenge is often the being physically present in events, meetings with galleries, marketing, PR, etc. I'm happy whenever I'm creating, but yes, that's the biggest challenge I often face: the need for marketing, physical presence, and PR.

AT: Who are some of your favorite, well known photographers? Why?

G.W.B: The ones who broke boundaries and stereotypes. The ones who keep being creative, expressing, giving us deep food for thoughts. To name a few: Edward Weston, R. Mapplethorpe, Mario Cravo Neto, Cristina Garcia Rodero, Alberto Garcia Alix, Eikoh Hosoe, Jungjin Lee, Laurent Millet, Sebastiao Salgado, Roger Ballen, Bernard Faucon, Duane Michals, Joel-Peter Witkin, and Jan Saudek.

AT: How much of your work is staged vs. spontaneous?

G.W.B: Most of my work is spontaneous, no matter whether it is self-portraits or with models, conceptual or nudes. I don't like to plan, I like to feel the moment and let it happen. They are more honest as well. And often more surprising.

AT: Why do you take photographs?

G.W.B: I do photography for the same reason as I write, paint, or draw: as a way to express myself. Which, for an autistic is probably the most challenging "obsession" or special interest. I stopped painting after I had a motorbike accident, as I was painting large scale and it required some physical strength and flexibility (hard to achieve with a spine hernia), so I turned towards photography, which became my main way of expression. But the two art forms are connected, as I often learn from painting to shoot and from shooting to paint.

AT: What do you find most challenging in photography?

G.W.B: Getting rid of the artistic blindness that keeps me emotionally connected with my work, so I can critically see it as a viewer. Being the eye, the subject, and the viewer simultaneously is challenging. That's why portfolio reviews are often useful.

AT: What advice would you give photographers starting out?

G.W.B: Visit ancient art museums and stare at old masters of painting: their sense of light and composition are the best to keep us creating. Then get out and shoot, shoot, shoot until you bleed from clicking. After that, get some emotional distance before printing or sharing them, so you can get rid of the artist blindness. ‡

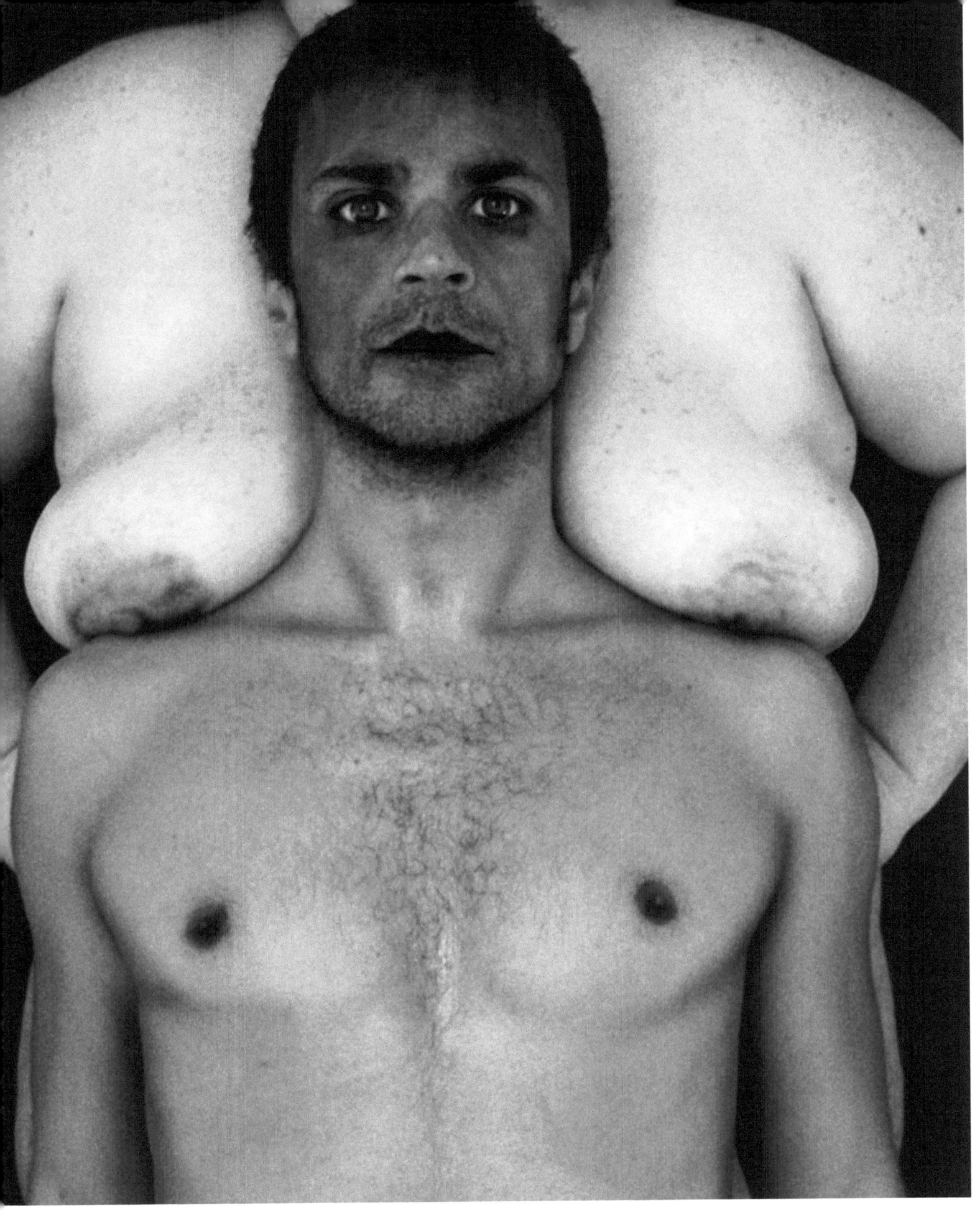

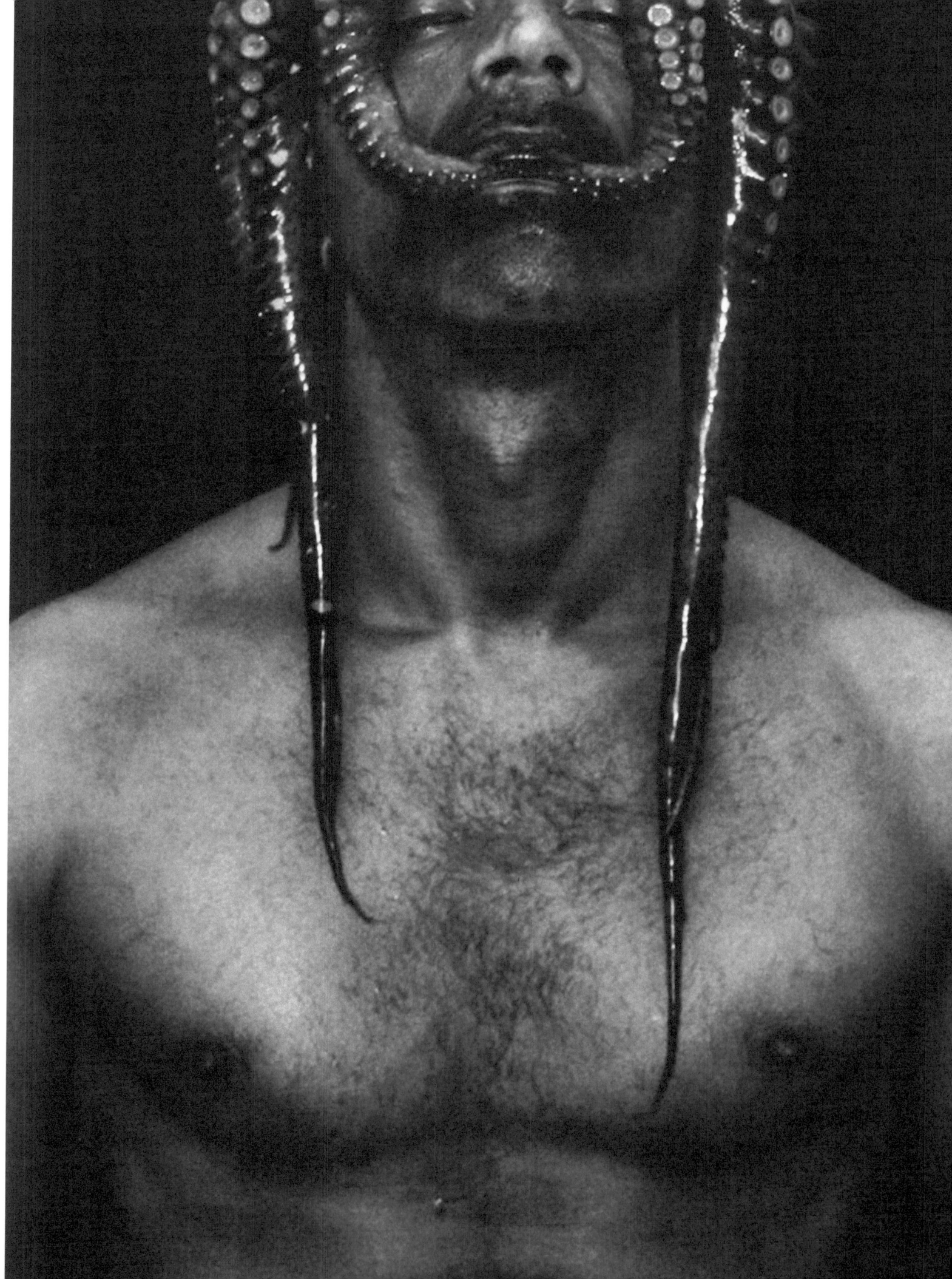

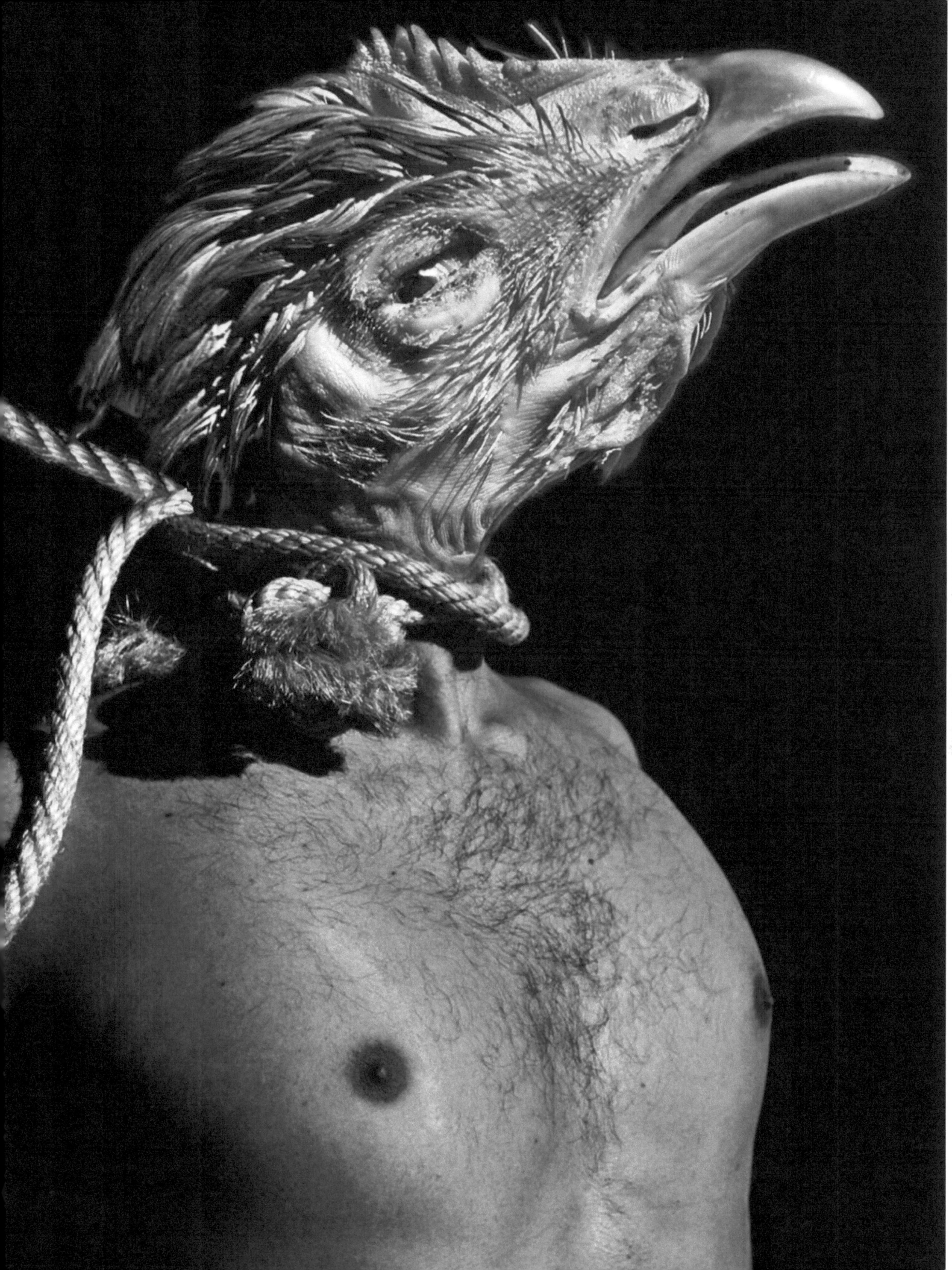

Brwax

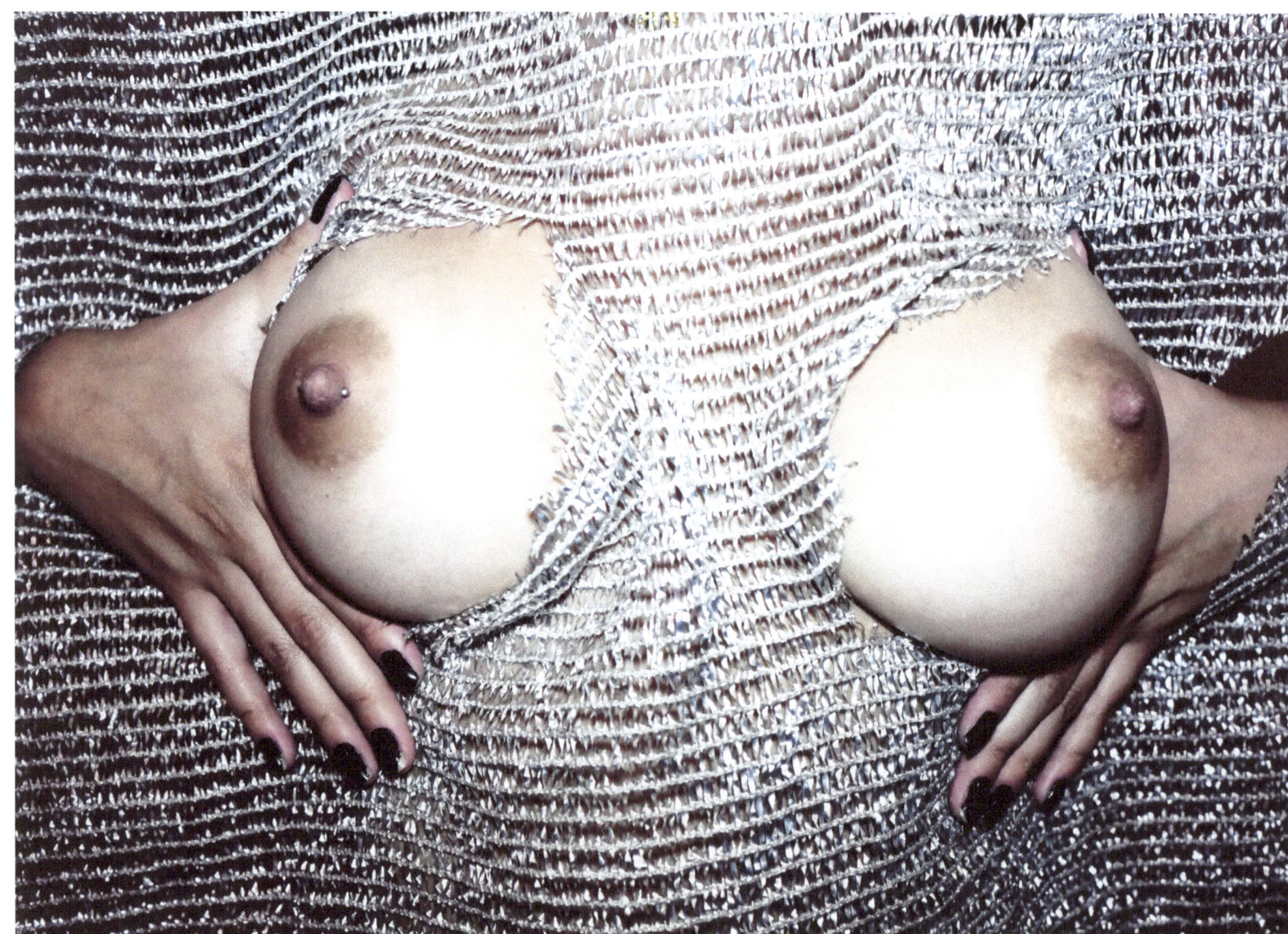

© Brwax pages 50-51

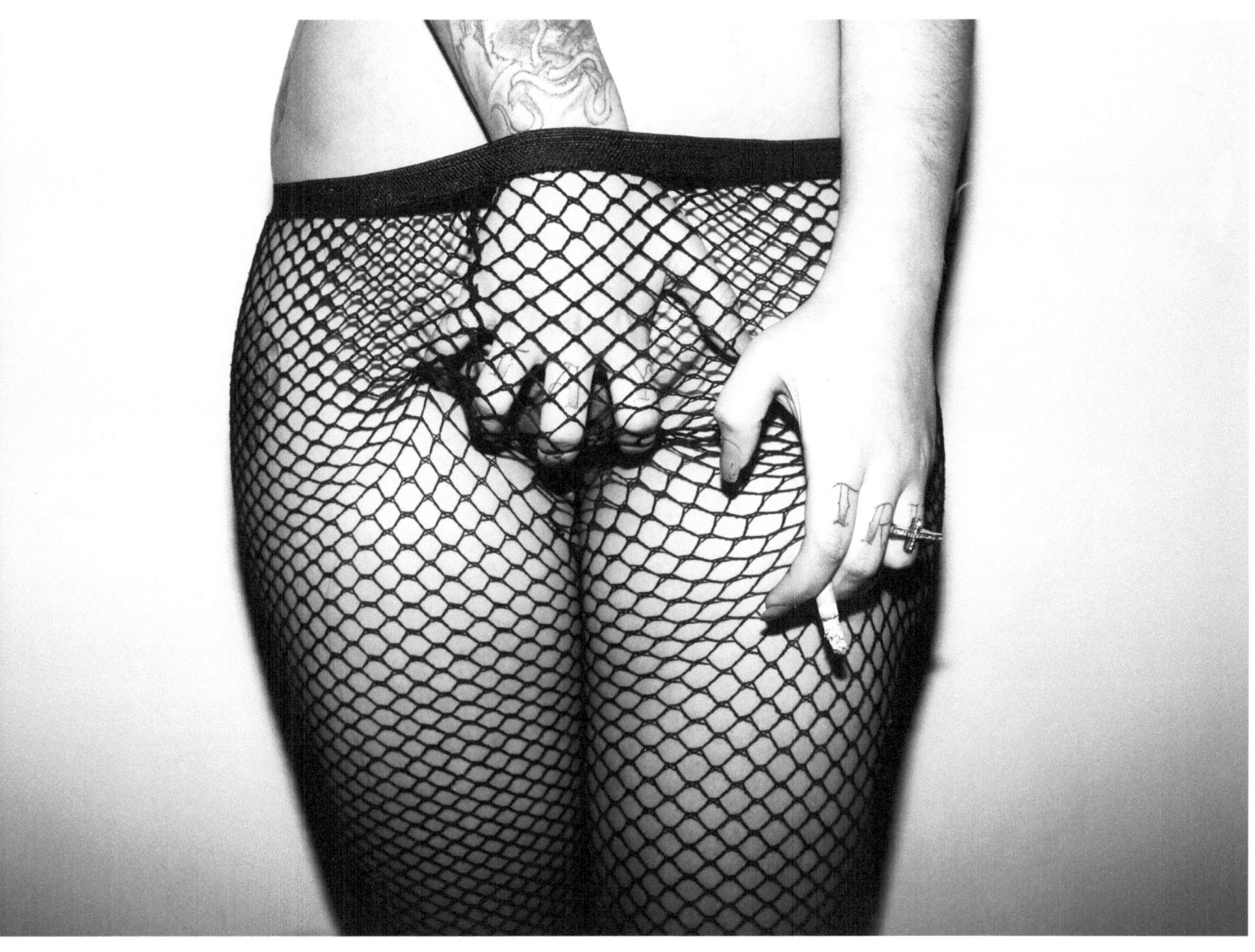

I began to shoot photographs around 5 years ago. I started with my girlfriends and friends of friends working at my house. I have now shifted to working in a collaborative complex of workmates where we share a huge studio space. With my gaining a foothold with my work, I realized I was becoming a professional. I had my own language and perspective, and slowly my work my work is being recognized. ‡

Mira Nedyalkova

I have always loved photography as art, but I started with drawing and modeling. In 2007, I discovered photography as a means to express myself and completely replaced painting. My photographs are not exactly photographs, because I edit a lot in Photoshop. My creations are somewhere in between paintings and photography. The two arts are, for me, very similar and interrelated. Frankly, the reason I chose photography was because I discovered Photoshop and the potential it brings. It is this unbelievable program that opened the way for me, the opportunity to continue creating, connecting painting and photography into one.

The majority of my works are in the water. This, of course, is not accidental. The water is my creation. The life, the power…the water is filled with tremendous energy. It is the winner of pleasure and delight, it gives life, but also poses a risk, a threat, it can destroy us.

I love the transparency and purity of water: light and reflecting and transformations that is suffered in contact with another medium.

For me, the water is highly erotic element precisely because of the opposites that brings. Water quenches our thirst and saves us. Water exemplifies the lust for life in each of us, the thirst for love and the eternal struggle and an attempt to erase, to dull, to heal the pain, sadness, and loneliness. ‡

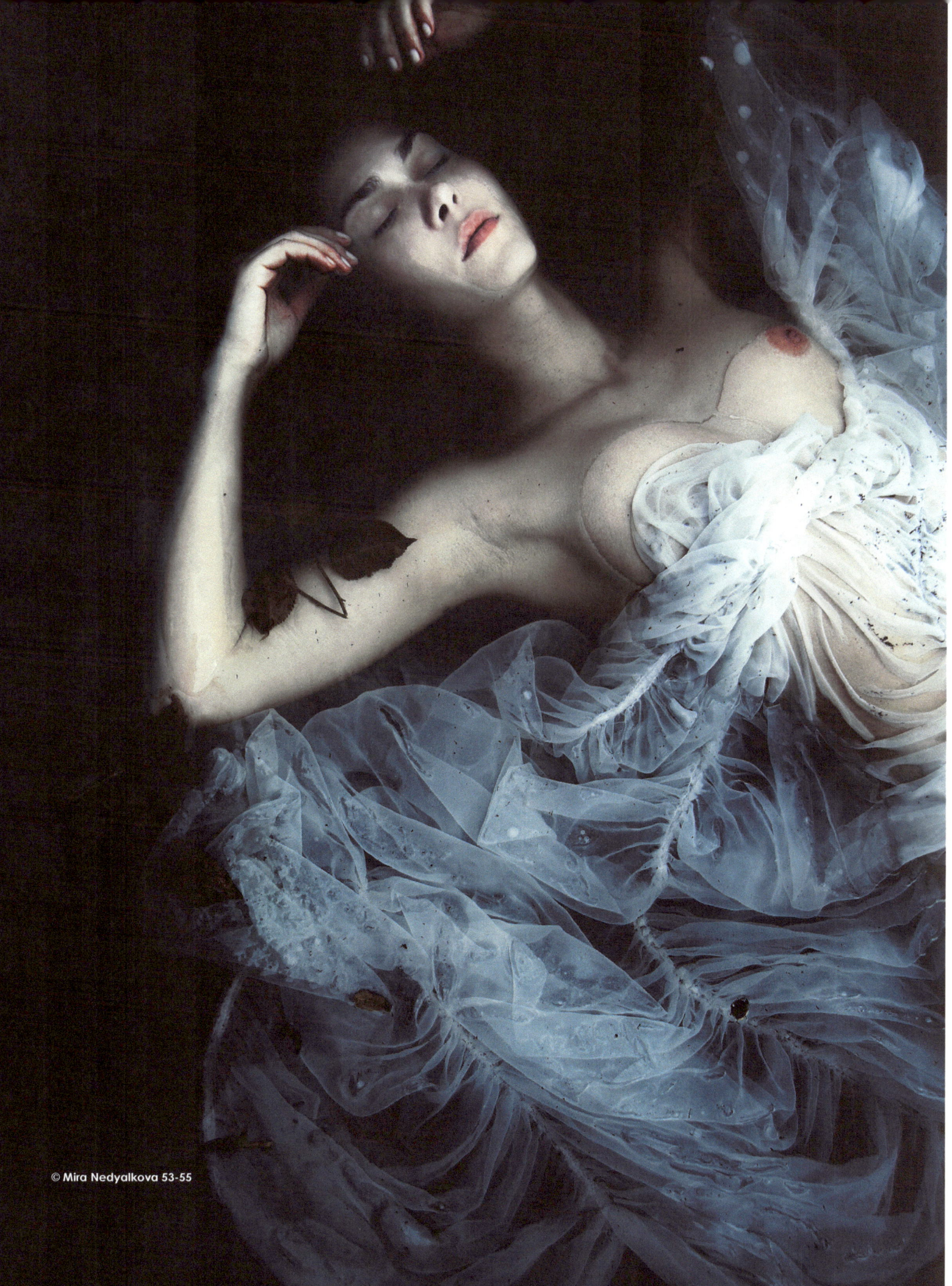

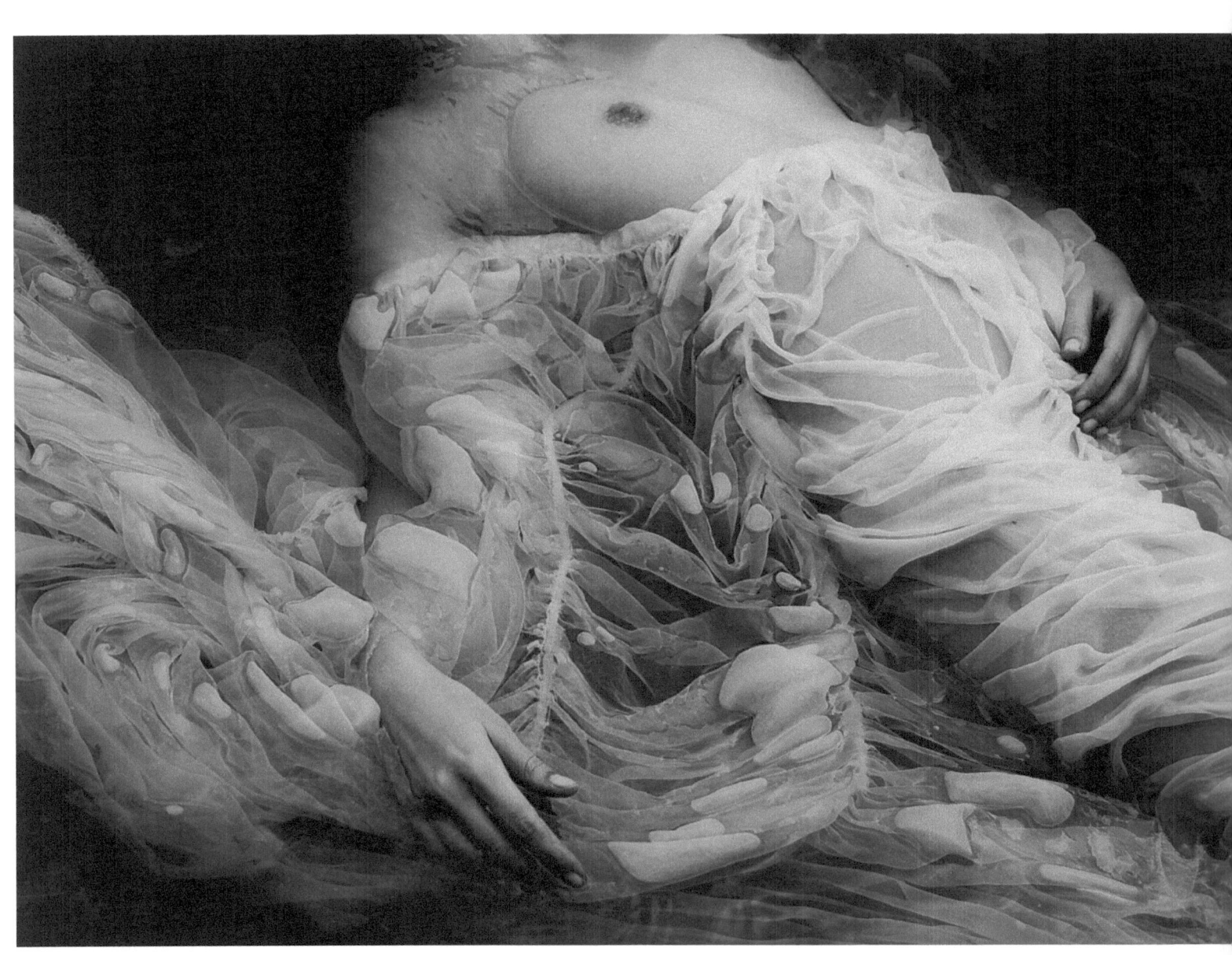

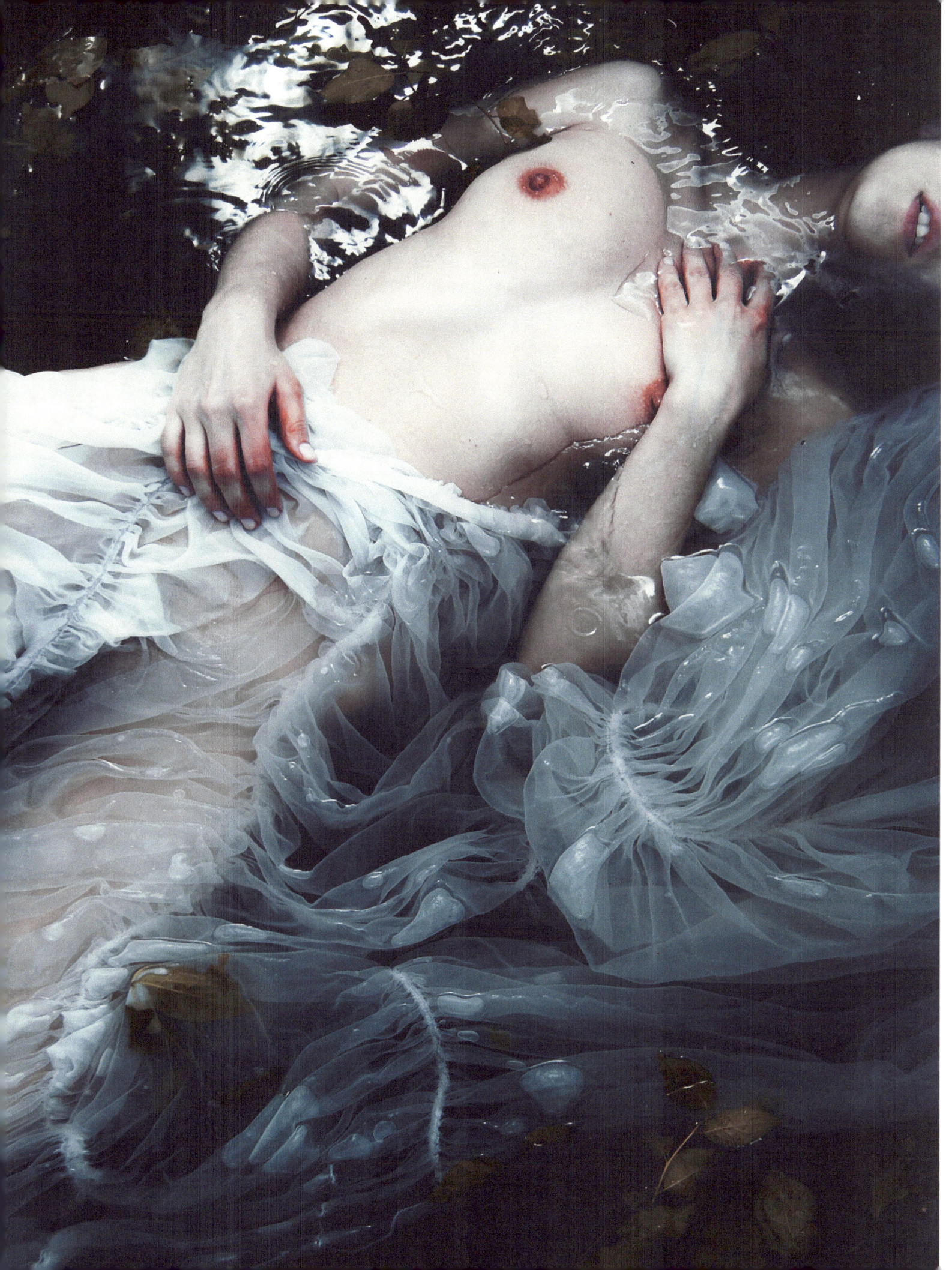

Nom de Guerre

Nom de Guerre is a US-based artist whose work is directed to abstract representations (photography & drawing) of the human figure, primarily addressing humanness in the modern world. In the course of doing this work, he also began shooting fashion and fashion nudes for the models with whom he worked on art projects. "It's a fun counterpoint to the heavier art work,"

Nom says, "but still requiring the focus and creativity that I use in my art. In my abstract artwork, form, light, and shadow are everything. In this work, I get to add in a narrative about a person – the model – whether it's an emotive headshot or sexy fashion nude. It's like getting to use both side of my brain." You can see more of his work at www.iamnomdeguerre.tumblr.com. ‡

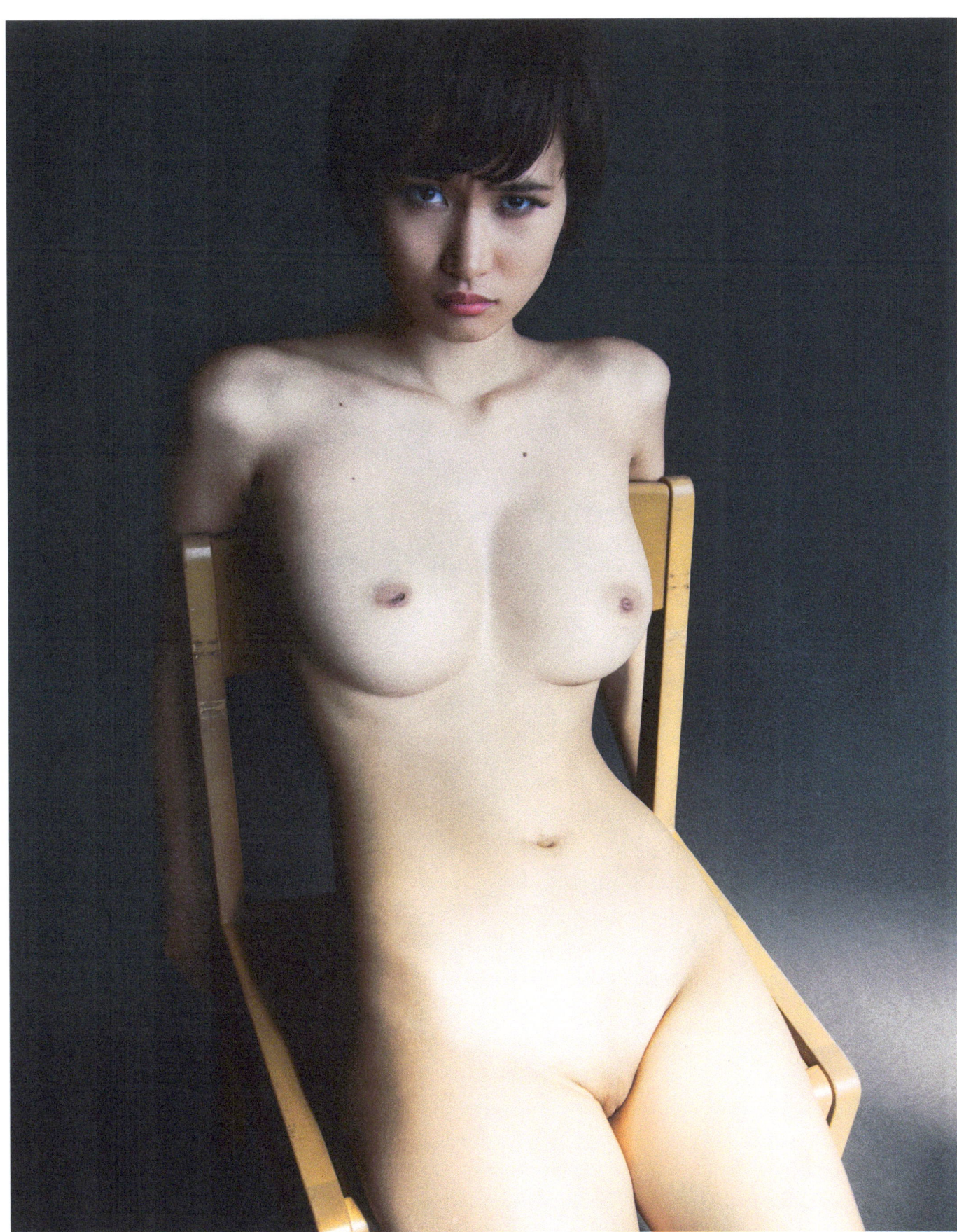

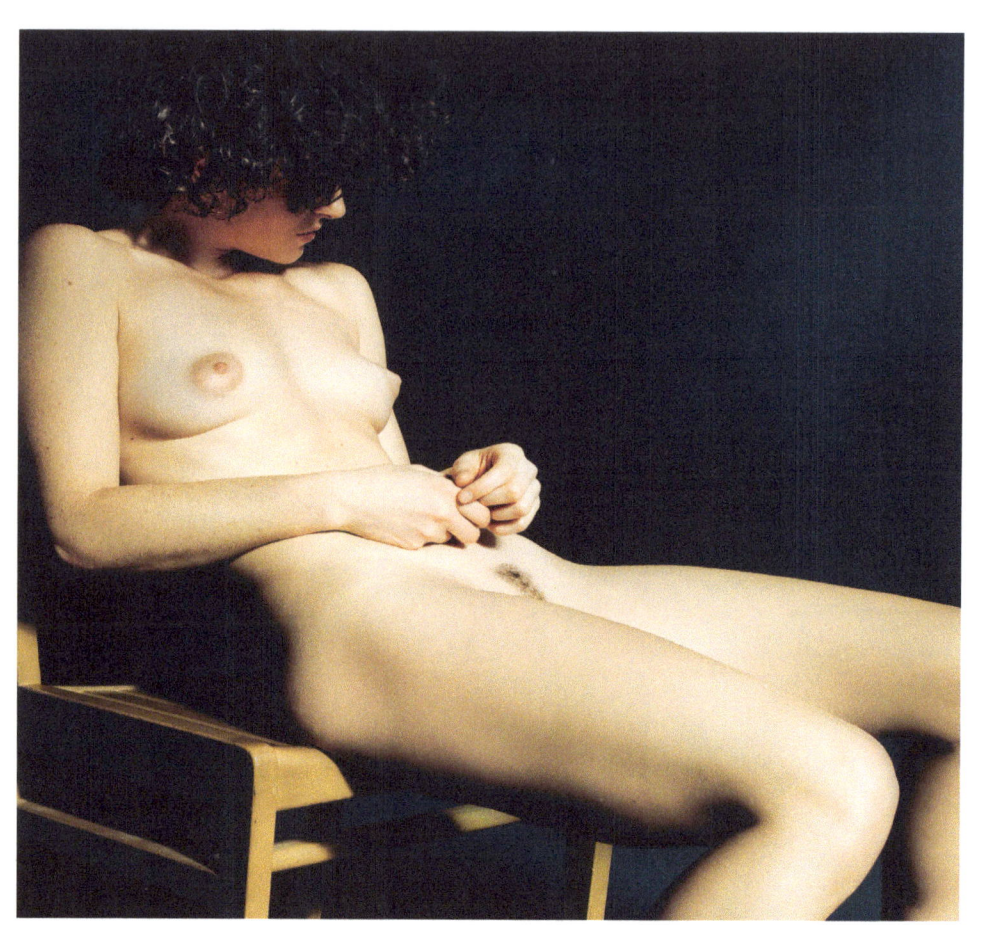

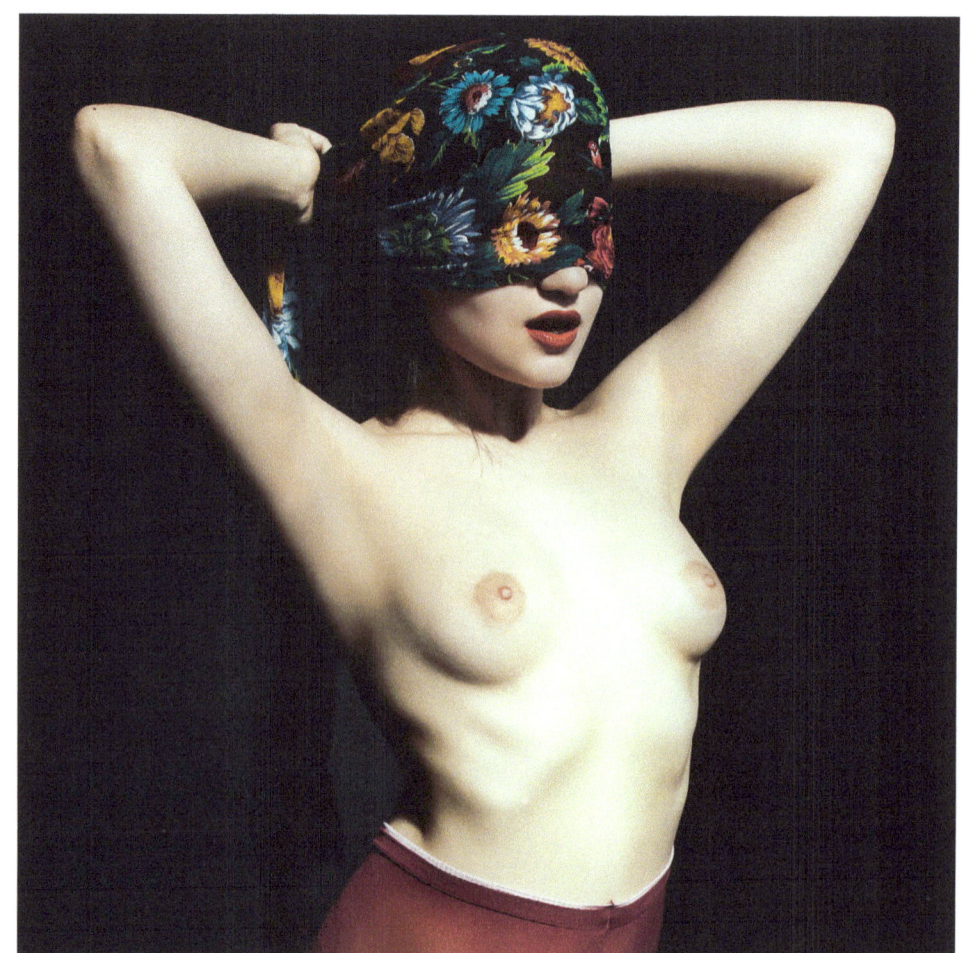

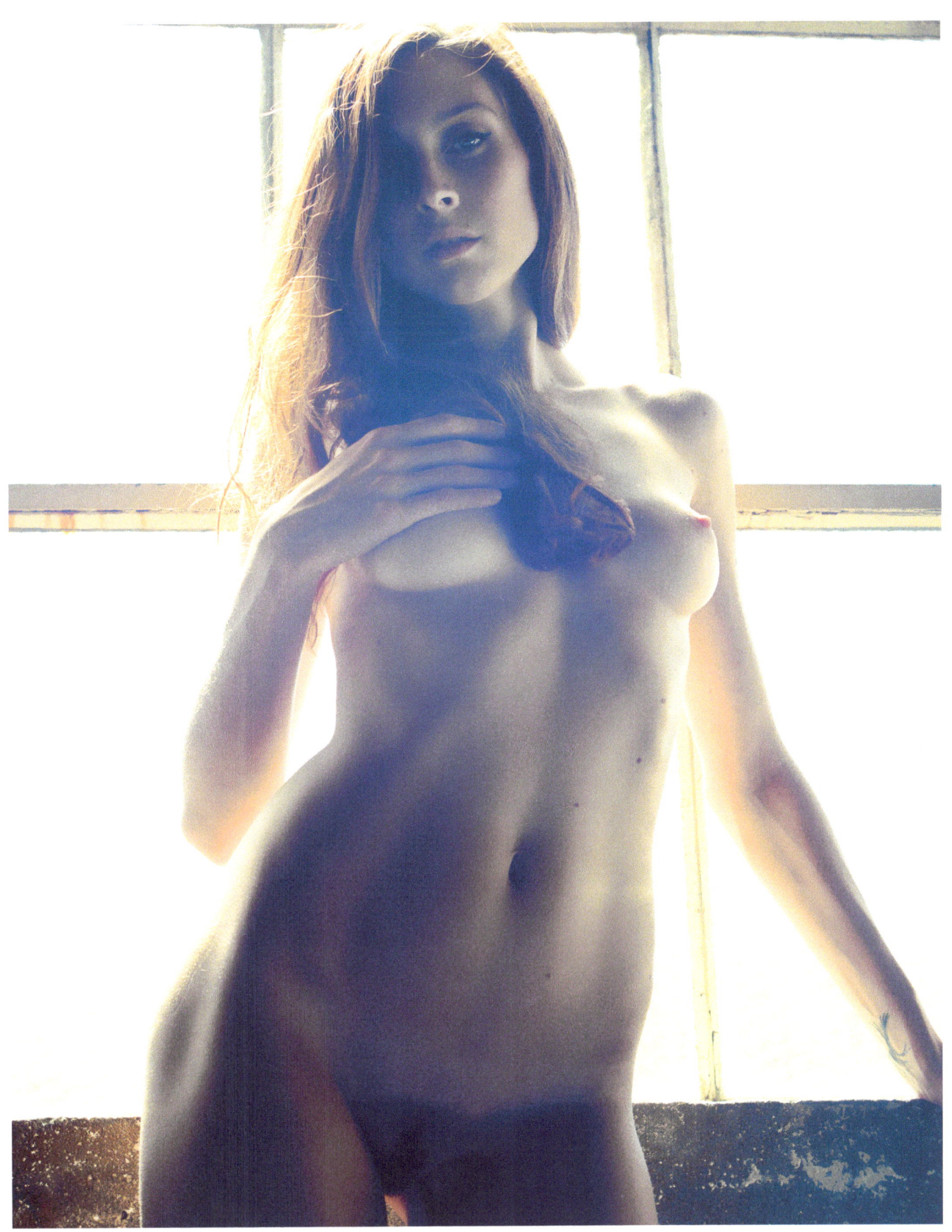

Curvology:
The Origins & Power of Female Body Shape
by David Bainbridge

Something remarkable has happened to women, something unique. Of all the creatures in the animal kingdom, human females stand out as having one special, powerful feature: curves. That may be good news for men, but it makes life complicated for women. Why do only human females have curves, how do they affect their lives, and why do they think about them so much? It was these simple questions which set David Bainbridge, a popular science writer and Cambridge anatomist and reproductive biologist, on a evolutionary, biological, psychological and socio-cultural quest to discover how female curviness lies at the centre of our species' success – what it means to be human, and what it means to be a woman.

Curvology follows an arc through human history, from the evidence of our ancestors' bones picked from the African dust, to the cult of the pre-clubbing selfie. One half of the members of our species live their lives in a body unlike any other in the animal kingdom, and this body exerts remarkable, pervasive effects on their movement, fertility, longevity, thought, mood, and even success.

Divided into ten chapters the book is a focused, novel, humane and accessible approach on the female body, rooted in the authors 'zoological' approach to this most distinctive aspect of human appearance.

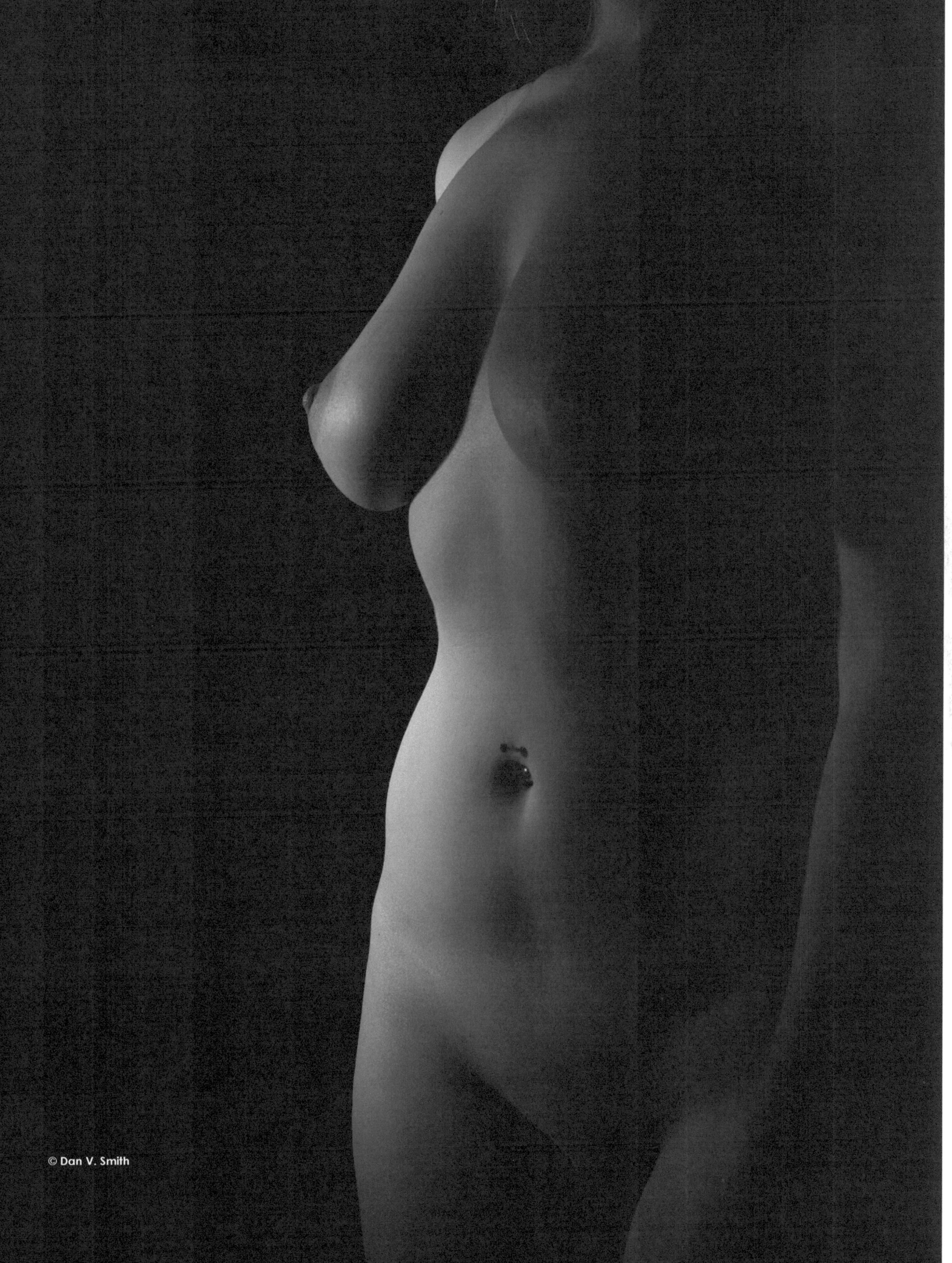

1. Where women's bodies came from

If women are unique in having waists, hips, bottoms and breasts, then why are they the only creature to have got that way? What were the forces which took our newly-bipedal species and completely reconfigured its females' bodies? Why do women need to have twice as much adipose tissue as men, why do they store it where they do, and what limitations does this put on them?

2. Where women's bodies come from

Female babies are not born curvy. In fact, apart from baby boys being slightly longer and leaner, the two sexes start off with remarkably similar body compositions. What are the processes which allow the wonderfully distinctive human female form to be re-made anew, as each girl grows up? Why do women's bodies vary so much? And how do girls feel about the fact that becoming womanly requires the accumulation of that much-vilified substance: fat?

3. The power of curves

Considering the powerful forces that have driven the evolution of female body shape, it is perhaps unsurprising how much it affects women's lives. However, only recently has it become evident that different curves exert different effects – adipose tissue in buttocks, bellies and breasts have different, and sometimes protective, effects on women's likelihood of suffering from killer-diseases such as diabetes, cancer and heart disease, as well as many other conditions. Also, the role of fat in female fertility now appears to be far more complex that we ever suspected.

4. What men want and why it doesn't matter

Because curves are so important in women's health, over the millennia men have evolved to be hard-wired to desire them. They 'know' that a curvy woman is most likely to provide them with healthy children – curvy daughters and curve-loving sons. So what exactly do men seek in a partner? How is the male brain programmed to lust after curves? Why are most men attracted to a wide variety of female body sizes but a relatively restricted set of body shapes? And have aeons of male lust sexually selected women to be more curvy than, strictly speaking, they need to be?

5. Trapped in a vessel of flesh

Does it feel different to inhabit a woman's body rather than a man's? Can we ever really know? Surprisingly, this age-old question is now being addressed by experts in psychology and robotics. For example, building thinking machines is showing us just how much the functioning of a brain is influenced by the shape of the physical 'body' in which it is located. And disorders in which people feel detached from their own body or even their own existence have started to show us how a woman's body may affect her sense of body-ownership, self and existence.

6. Comfort and discomfort eating

For 99.9% of human existence, we have been scrabbling around to find food, but now all that has changed. We have brains designed for starvation, but the world around us overflows with calories. For women the dilemmas are particularly stark – from a young age they learn to restrain their appetites, to prepare food for others rather than themselves, and that 'small is attractive'. Food means health and disease, comfort and guilt, being small and being curvy. Can these conflicts ever be resolved?

7. A malaise of shapes

How did our species get to the point where large numbers of us, mostly female, starve and binge their way to death, sickness and serious injury? What are eating disorders, and why do some of us get them but not others? When did we start getting them – are they a new thing, or as old as our species? Most of all, what strange evolutionary forces lie behind our propensity to suffer eating disorders, and were those forces once beneficial rather than harmful?

8. Following the fashion

Men may be irrevocably hard-wired to desire certain core elements of the female form, but what about humans' more transient preferences for women's shapes? Why is a body size or shape deemed attractive in London or California but thought ugly in Nigeria? Why was heroin chic replaced by Sophie Dahl and Beyoncé? Why does thinness become the body-ideal in certain places in certain decades? And what is the actual evidence that the media really do influence women's opinions of their own bodies?

9. Covering up and tucking in

Clothes, shoes, jewellery, depilation, piercing, tattooing, and now surgery. Far more than the male, the female body is seen as something to be concealed, exposed, altered, corrected and accentuated. Why do we think this? When do girls learn it? And how, exactly, do women do it? This chapter includes a radical new theory of what each and every item of female clothing is actually designed to achieve. It also investigates how surgery, once synonymous with treating severe disease, became an acceptable form of body enhancement.

10. Why women care and why it's complicated

Throughout the book, the theme emerges that the central biological role of female curvaceousness in our species has led to it becoming built into every aspect of human life – women's health, their sense of self, men's desire, control of eating and guilt, body fashions and fashion for bodies. Finally, the author addresses the question of why women think about their bodies so much, and in such complex ways. The Darwinian idea that they wish to impress men is soon discounted, and instead the true reasons why body shape is central to female life and individual life-success are laid bare. ‡

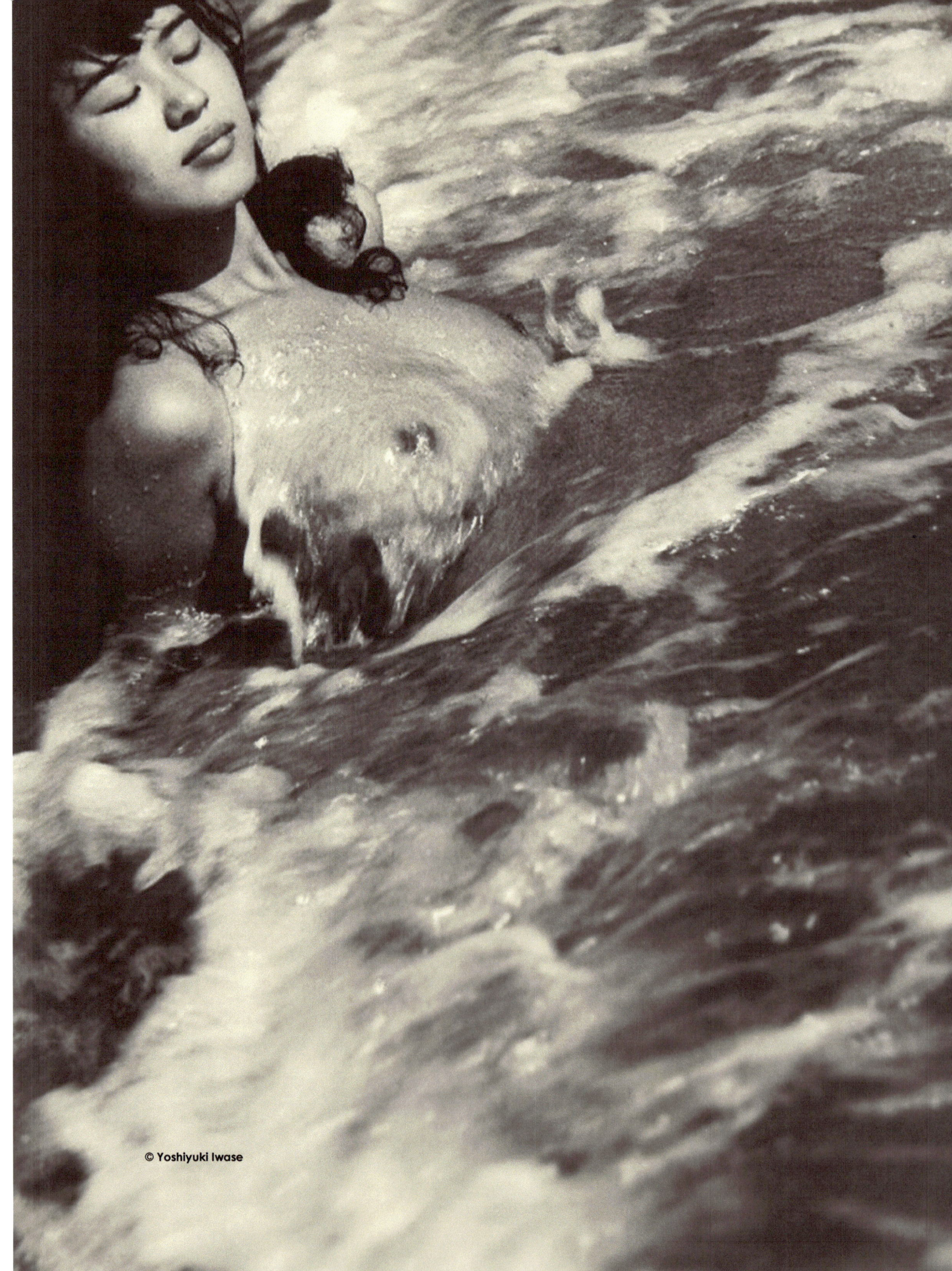

© Yoshiyuki Iwase

Ama

The Pearl Diving Mermaids of Japan

By Michael Gakuran

One of the lesser-known but fascinating parts of Japanese culture is that of the Ama pearl divers. Ama literally means 'woman of the sea' and is recorded as early as 750 in the oldest Japanese anthology of poetry, the Man'yoshu. These women specialised in freediving some 30 feet down into cold water wearing nothing more than a loincloth. Utilising special techniques to hold their breath for up to 2 minutes at a time, they would work for up to 4 hours a day in order to gather abalone, seaweed and other shellfish.

The most profitable pursuit however was diving for pearls. Traditionally for Ama, finding a pearl inside an oyster was akin to receiving a large bonus while they went about their ancestral practice of collecting shellfish. That changed when Kokichi Mikimoto, founder of Mikimoto Pearl, began his enterprise.

Mikimoto used Ama divers to look after his cultivated pearls on Mikimoto Pearl Island, near Toba city. This business was the main reason for the strong association between Ama and pearl diving among foreign observers that continues to this day. Another little-known fact is that the 'traditional' white attire we often see Ama divers wearing was also created by Mikimoto. He observed how surprised the foreign tourists visiting his pearl island were when seeing the Ama diving naked wearing only their traditional loincloth.

The role of the Mikimoto Ama was to collect the oysters from the seabed so that the pearl-producing nucleus could be inserted. Once this critical process was completed, the Ama then carefully returned the oysters to the seabed – in a place where they were protected from external dangers (such as typhoons and red tide).

In order to successfully complete this process, each diver would have to hold her breath for up to two minutes at a time in often freezing cold waters. Upon surfacing, the Ama opened their mouths slightly and exhaled slowly, making a whistling sound known as 'Isobue'.

While traditional Ama divers wore only a fundoshi (loincloth) to make it easier to move in the water and a tenugui (bandanna) around their head to cover their hair, Mikimoto Ama wore a full white diving costume and used a wooden barrel as a buoy. They were connected to this buoy by a rope and would use it to rest and catch their breath between dives.

Although the tradition is still maintained across many parts of Japan, the skinny-dipping practices of old have largely been lost. Since the Meiji era, divers wore goggles for clarity and in 1964, rubbery, black wetsuits were introduced.

One photographer in particular stands out with his photographs of the Ama. His name was Yoshiyuki Iwase (1904-2001). He was given a gift of a small Kodak camera when young and found his muse in the beautiful mermaids of the tired, coastal regions of Japan. Thanks to his efforts, we can take a step back in time and have a glimpse at what life was like working as an Ama diver, and also see his progression as a photographer moving into nude portraits. Since his website is now offline, I'm gathering up as many vintage pictures as I can for posterity that I'll post as its own separate article soon.

One of the reasons Ama are largely female is said to be their thicker layer of fat than their male counterparts to help them endure the cold water during long periods of diving. Another reason is the self-supporting nature of the profession, allowing women to live independently and foster strong communities. Perhaps most surprisingly however, is the old age to which these women are able to keep diving. Most Ama are elderly women (some even surpassing 90 years of age) who have practiced the art for many, many years, spending much of their life at sea.

With lack of young women to succeed their elders and modernisation of Japan's fisheries however, this ancient practice is dwindling. Numbers have dropped to just 1/8th of what they once were. In 1956 there were 17,611 Ama in Japan but as of 2010 only 2,174 remained. Of those, 973 (nearly half) work in either Toba or Shima city, Mie prefecture.

As technology progressed, the Ama communities were faced with decisions – adopt new tools and equipment or retain traditions? One of the most important parts of the decision-making was the consideration of sustainability. New fishing methods could easily enable greater hauls and reduce work, but at the same time, increase the risk of overfishing and damaging the delicate ecosystems that supported life for these coastal towns. Rules were introduced to prevent this.

On Hegura island in Wajima city, rules state that abalone under 10 centimetres must be returned to the sea, with a punishment of two days without work if caught breaking them. Despite their efforts however, numbers of abalone and other shellfish have been in decline, in part due to overfishing, but also the rising sea temperatures which affects the growth of seaweed the shellfish eat.

This culture of national mermaids diving for the nation is not unique to Japan. Since 2007, Korea has been presenting its best case to have the Haenyo divers of Jeju Island listed as a UNESCO Intangible Cultural Heritage. In similar fashion, Japan has now joined the races by recommending its own female divers, boosted by the popularity of a recent NHK drama 'Amachan,' starring a young girl who moves to the Tohoku region of Japan to became an Ama diver.

Although perhaps the scantily-clad, romanticised image of the profession is a thing of the past, there's still a rich history and culture that needs to be conveyed to younger generations. The tourism industry at Mikimoto Pearl is a great start to help preserve the memory, but the age-old fishing traditions held by small coastal villages are definitely in need of special attention to make sure their heritage isn't forgotten completely. ‡

Polar
Ester

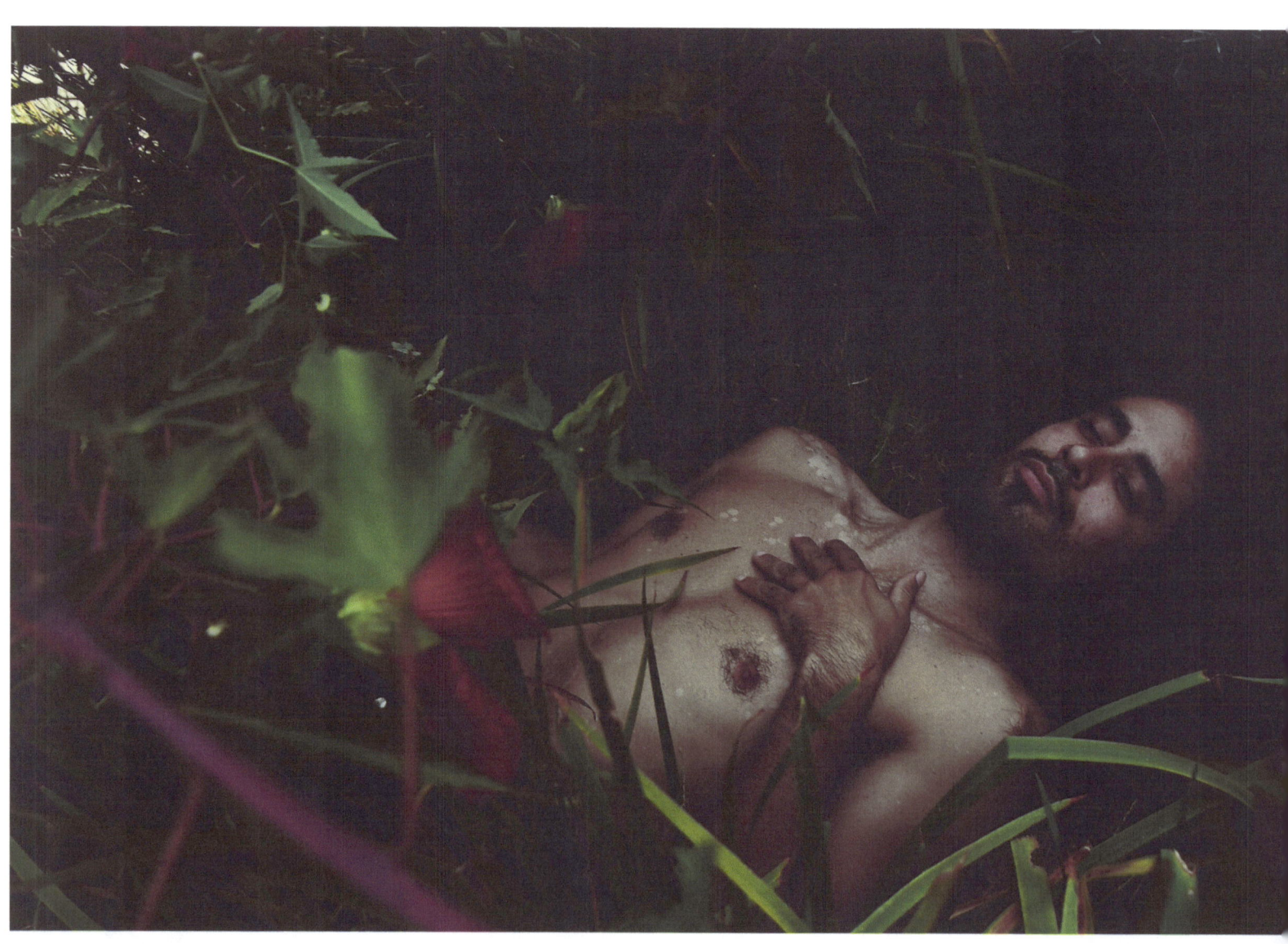

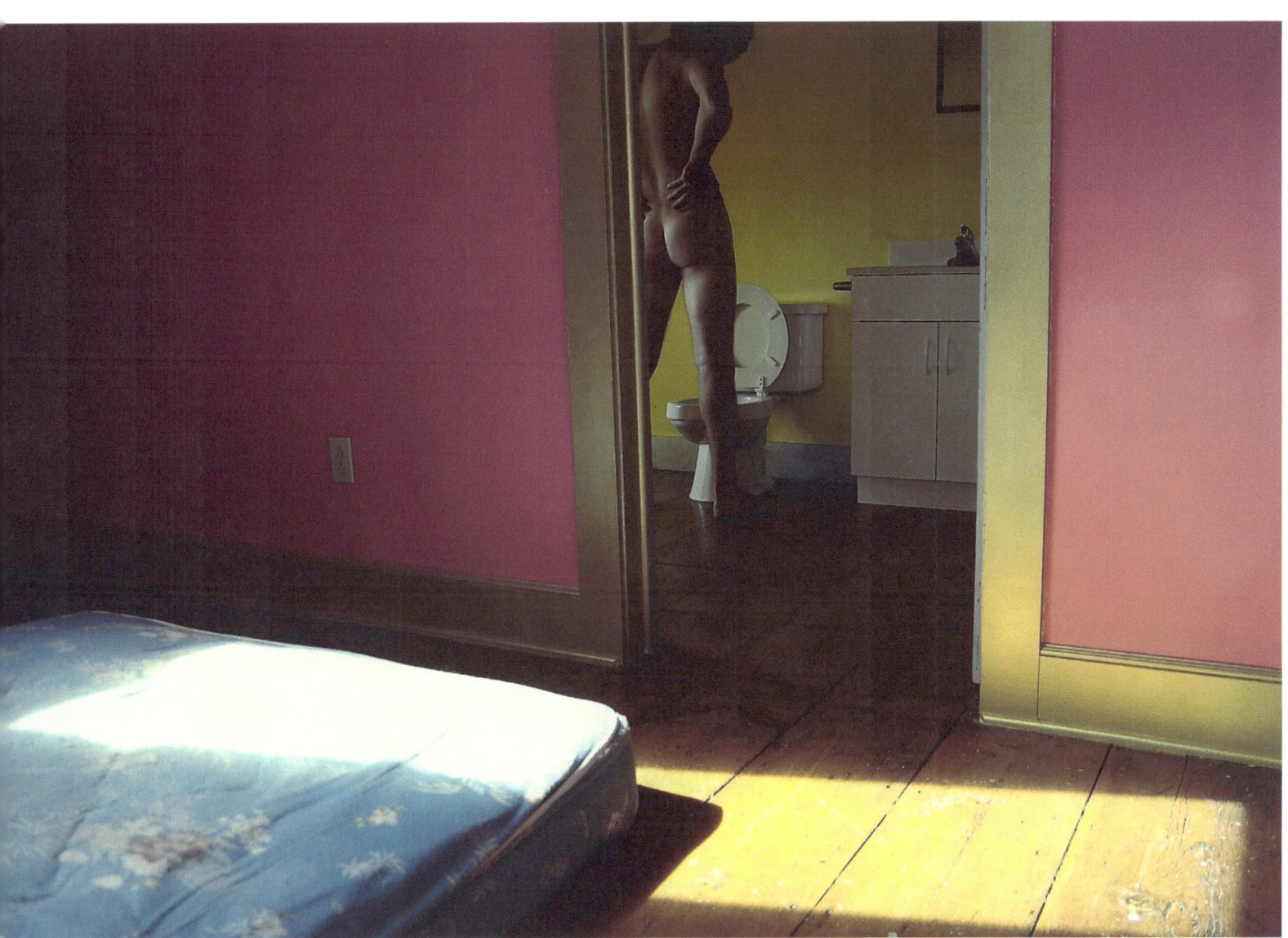

My name is Pola Esther. I was born in Poland. Legend says I was kissed by the Pope and that event made me who I am. As an artist I use photography as my main platform for expression. I like to photograph nature, mostly human. In my work I reflect on my intimacy, femininity, and sexuality. I respond intensely to my close surroundings, approaching it with a poetic, eager, and sometimes ironic eye. I'm constantly looking for visual fantasy in commodities. I'm not only searching for beauty in its given form but also in its peculiar dimensions. I often challenge my subjects to reach towards extraordinary aspects of their personality to achieve certain social commentary and reaction in a personal way. I have a background in theater and use its action and dynamic energy in my concepts and presentations. I'm always ready to play and experiment with the endless variations of people, places, and things - this is the spirit which drives my creativity. ‡

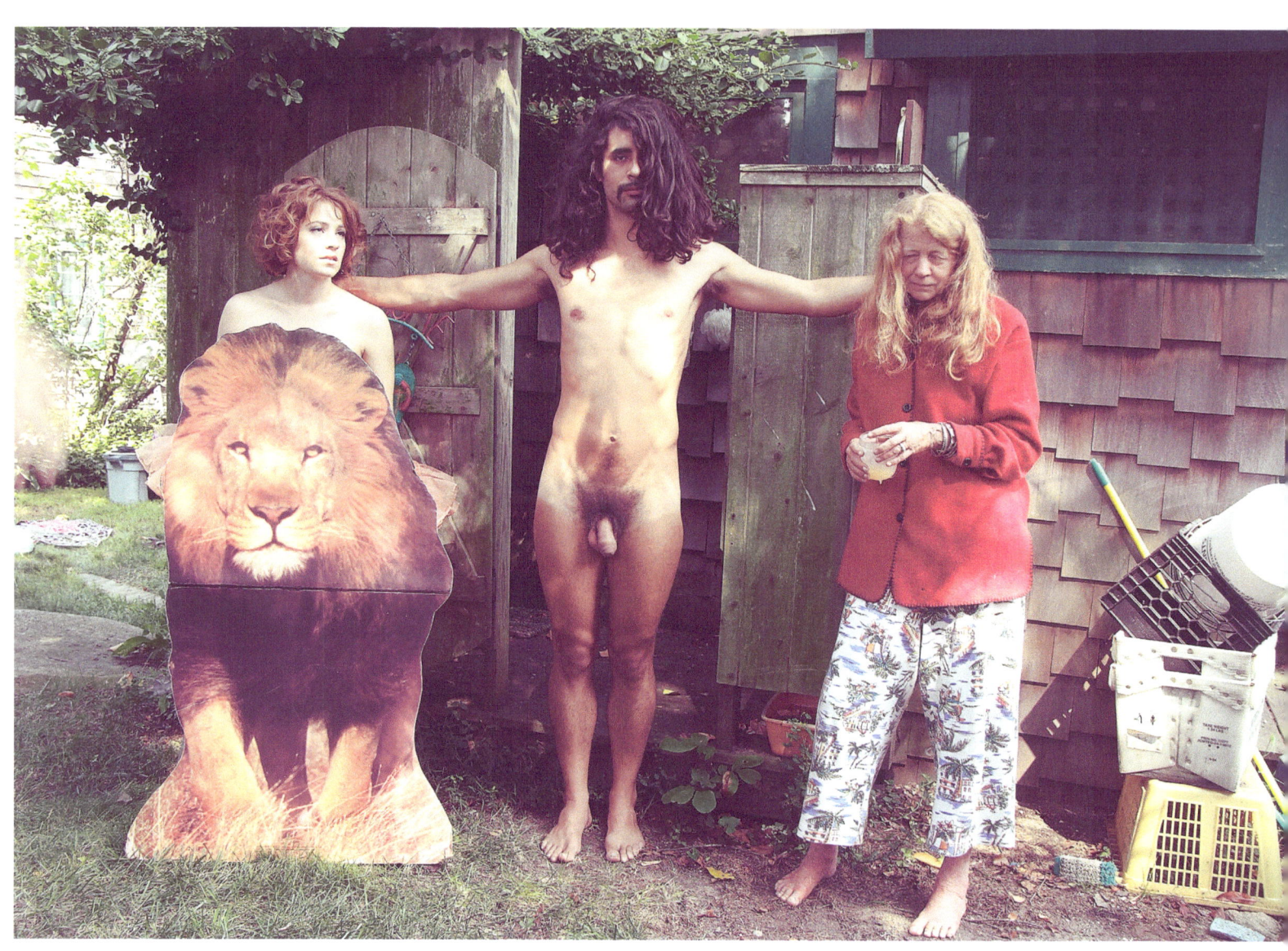

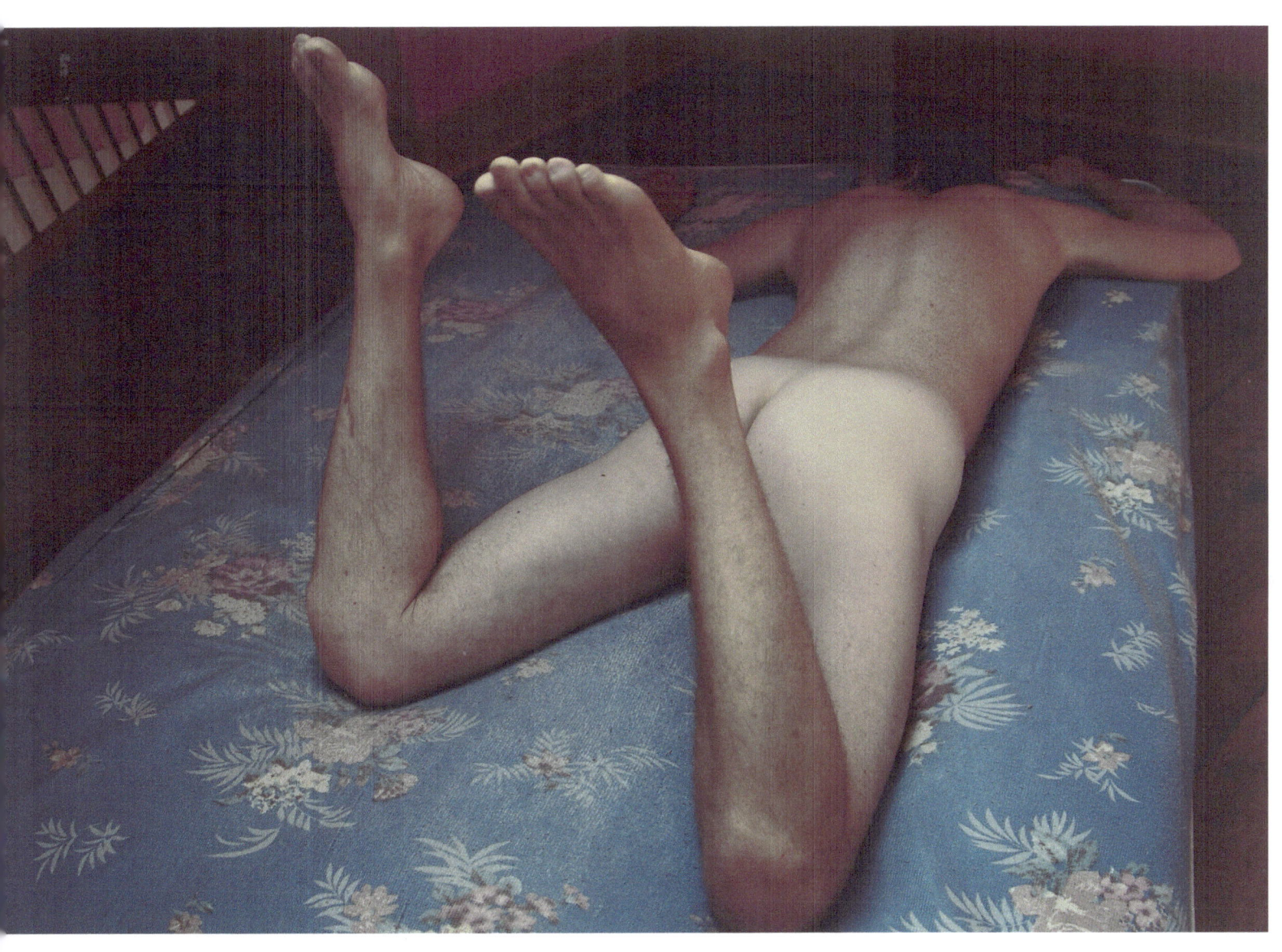

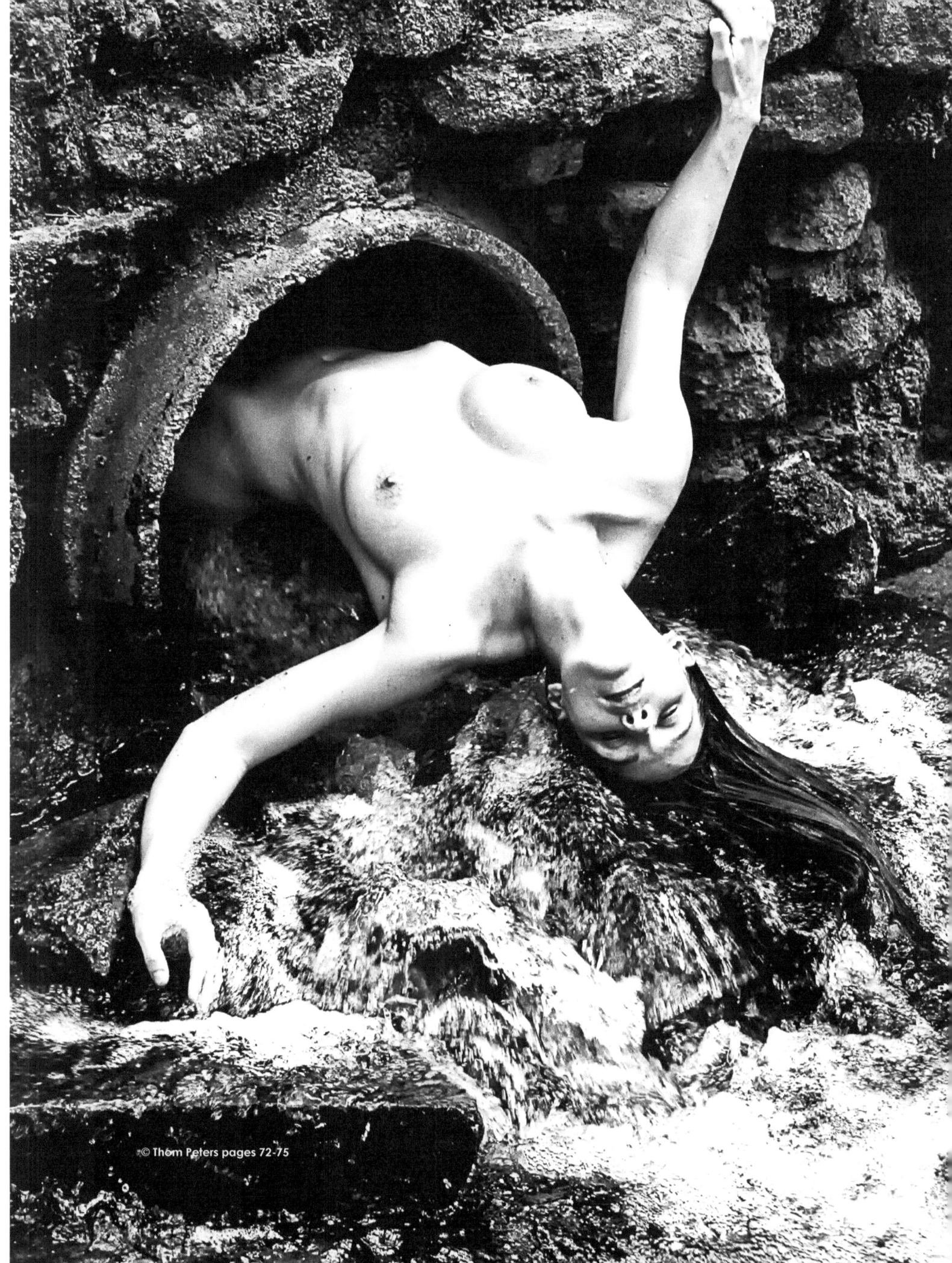

THOM PETERS

My focus is the creation of beautiful artistic nudes. The following quote reflects my attitude on shooting artistic nudes better than anything I could devise:

"If I have chosen the female form in particular, it is because beauty has been debased, and exploited in our sensual twentieth century. We seem to have a need to turn innocent nature into evil ugliness by the twist of the mind. Woman has been target of much that is sordid and cheap, especially in photography. To raise, to elevate, to endorse with timeless reverence the image of woman, has been my mission – the reason for my work."
—Ruth Bernhard, from "Views on Nudes" by Bill Jay

My current focus is Art Nudes, mostly in black and white with some color photos, shot outdoors, indoors, and in the studio. I look to present the human form in an artistic manner that is creative, beautiful, and honors the beauty and humanity in all of us. I DO NOT shoot erotica or fetish. While some of my photos may have a sensual undertone, this is usually due to the personality of the model.

I generally choose my shooting locations based on aspects of the model and the memory that will be evoked in a scene by those surroundings. In the studio, I light my models in such a way that the image demands the attention of the viewer. I accomplish this using female art models in classic poses or while performing dance moves as backlit silhouettes. Props in simple forms are often used indoors to assist models in posing as statuesque figures of classic form and beauty. I also use rooms as backdrops to scenes with furniture, wood floors, and painted walls that will engage the viewer and focus exclusively on the human form I'm representing. These studio elements provide a balanced and graceful staging for each moment on film. My outdoor work seeks to use the texture and contrast in tones between the natural world and that of human skin. Natural forms in the scene allow the models to mimic or further accentuate the beauty around them. Bringing the human form back to nature allows me to see the balance of the forms together. The contrast of the indoor photos is that the human form is singular, or it is the contrast to the manmade props of scene.

I've been photographing professionally for 10+ years. However, I've been photographing for nearly 35 years with everything from a Kodak Brownie to my Canon 50D today. I absolutely love photography and pushing my boundaries of creativity. It is the medium which fits my inner voice. While much of my work is now digital in nature, I also shoot medium format film with my Rollicord, primarily using Ilford film.

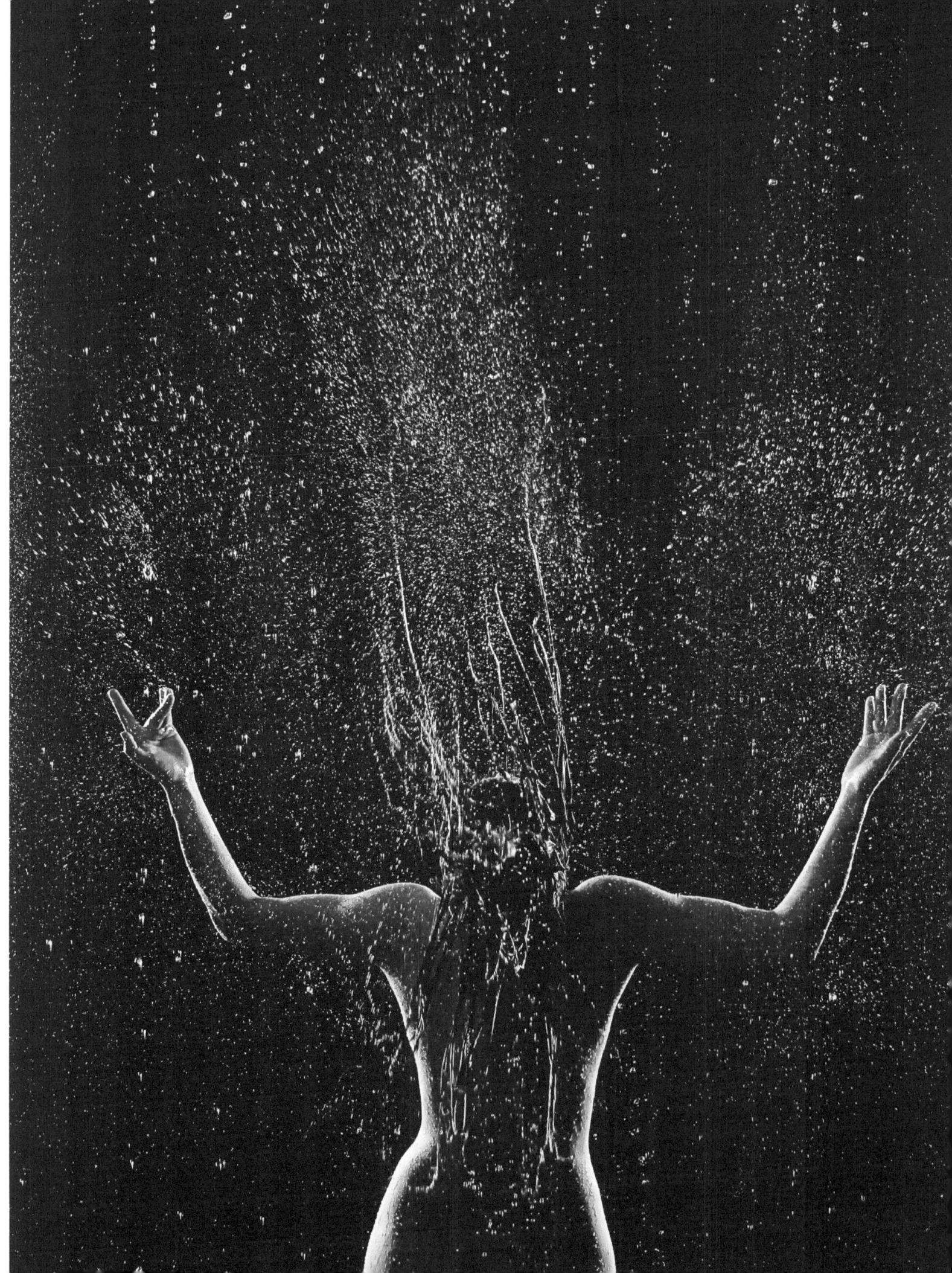

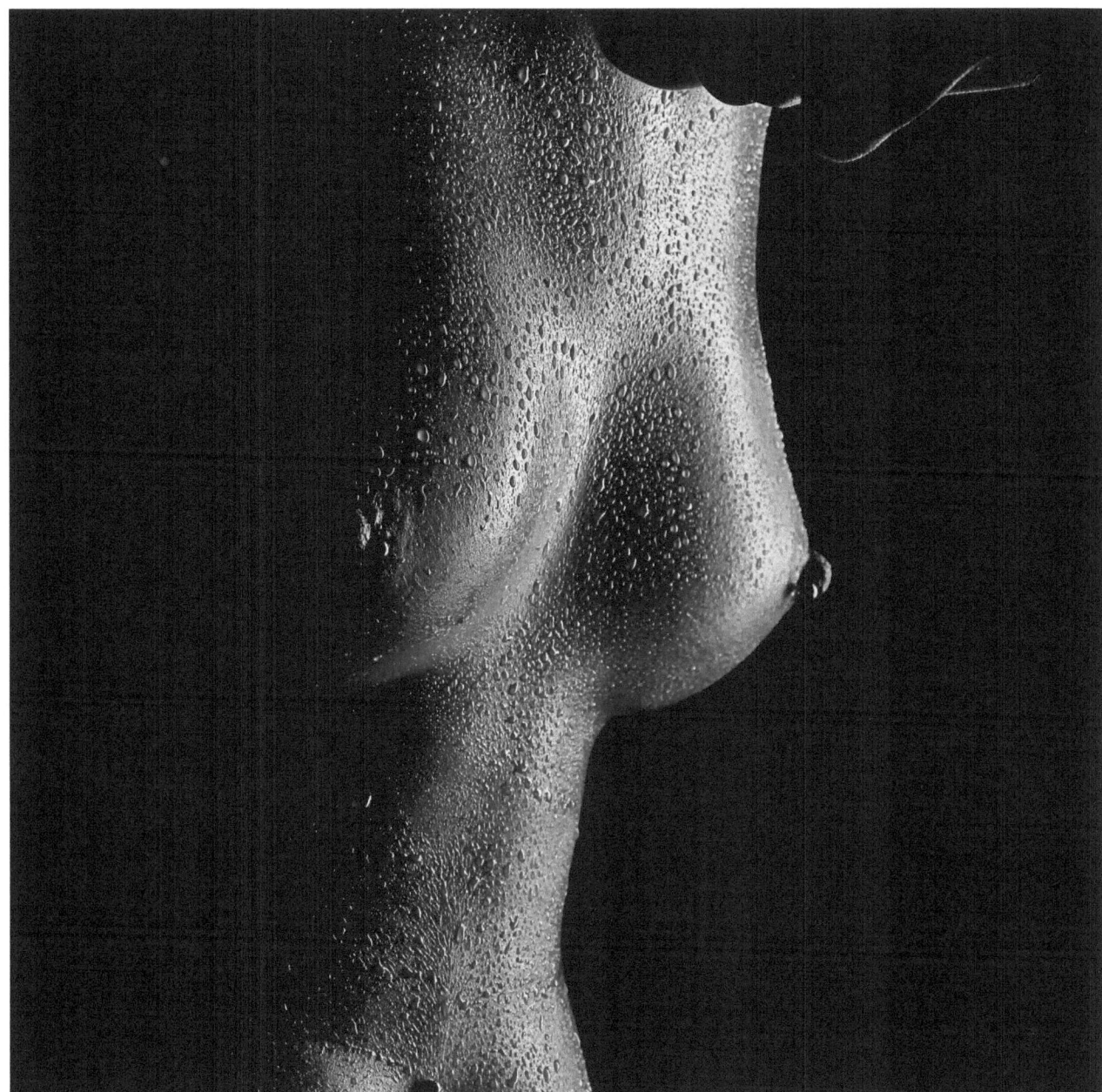

For my digital work, I rely on Lightroom 3, and Photoshop CS5. I also use Nik Software Silver EFX Pro for my black and white conversions. My workflow consists of selection and initial adjustments of images in Lightroom, continued conversion to B&W, with adjustments in Silver EFXPro, and final adjustments, cosmetic corrections and sharpening in Photoshop. For film work I rely on commercial development firms for processing and printing my images. For some projects I am able to develop, enlarge, and print film work myself at a local Art Institute darkroom facility.

The primary uses of my photography are for public art exhibitions, art contests (such as ArtPrize), and publication. ‡

More of my work can be seen at:
http://pixelperfectphotography.com.